A PASTOR'S TOOLBOX

A Pastor's Toolbox

Management Skills for Parish Leadership

Edited by Paul A. Holmes

LITURGICAL PRESS
Collegeville, Minnesota

www.litpress.org

1   2   3   4   5   6   7   8   9

Library of Congress Cataloging-in-Publication Data

A pastor's toolbox : management skills for parish leadership / edited by Paul A. Holmes.
    pages   cm
   ISBN 978-0-8146-3808-8 — ISBN 978-0-8146-3833-0
   1. Pastoral theology—Catholic Church.   2. Christian leadership—Catholic Church.
  3. Parishes.   I. Holmes, Paul A., editor of compilation.

BX1913.P348 2014
254—dc23   2013037427

Contents

Preface

Thomas J. Healey

It is both a pleasure and honor to prepare this preface to *A Pastor's Toolbox: Management Skills for Parish Leadership*. Above all, it's a chance to provide readers with some history and context around the Toolbox for Pastoral Management initiative and to thank the many committed and talented people who worked so hard to bring this first-of-its-kind program, and now its companion handbook, to life.

The idea for this handbook came to me like a bolt out of the blue—or was it the heavens?—as I sat at Mass in a Jesuit church in San Francisco about five years ago. The fact that I should have been praying is beside the point. Because we were having some problems getting the Toolbox for Pastoral Management off the ground as quickly as we wanted, I realized we were depriving many new pastors of a valuable learning opportunity. So, *why not do a book in the meantime?* Why not fill the void with a valuable resource based on Toolbox presentations that new pastors—who are the first to admit they didn't go to the seminary to learn business skills—could readily and conveniently draw on? The resource could be a sort of how-to guide designed to strengthen pastors' critical skill sets in church administration, finance, and personnel management.

Enter Fr. Paul Holmes, professor of servant leadership at Seton Hall University. A high-energy type as anyone who knows him will attest, Fr. Holmes took the book concept and prepared an exhaustive list of temporal administration topics that needed to be covered. With the creative and intellectual input of Michael Brough from the National Leadership Roundtable on Church Management and Jim Lundholm-Eades, director of parish services and planning for the Archdiocese of Saint Paul and Minneapolis, the project began to jell. The only thing missing was the

Toolbox seminars themselves to provide content. Fortunately, those sessions were soon launched, and after we had completed three weeklong, face-to-face workshops—all judged unqualified successes by everyone involved—we knew we had a green light for our book. To that end, many of the wide-ranging seminar modules were edited and adapted to the appropriate format, and earnest discussions began with Liturgical Press. The result of that process is what you now hold in your hands.

As for the umbrella Toolbox for Pastoral Management program, the story begins with Lt. Gen. James Dubik, who was in charge of accelerating the training of all the military services and police forces in Iraq and Afghanistan before retiring from the U.S. Army. Lt. Gen. Dubik decided to channel his extraordinary training experience in an entirely different direction: creating a skills-based program for new pastors that would emulate the work of the Leadership Roundtable (of which Jim is an active member) in the areas of finance, personnel, and planning.

The next step was to take that seedling to Seton Hall University, which over the past quarter-century had earned a global reputation for the continuing education of priests through its International Institute for Clergy Formation. We sat down with Msgr. Robert Sheeran, president of Seton Hall, and Kurt Borowsky, chair of Seton Hall's board of regents, to determine if their university had the resources and interest to explore an executive education program for new pastors, similar in concept to those run by many of the nation's top business schools. Msgr. Sheeran was indeed interested and asked us to check back in a month. We did and found ourselves in the company of Fr. Holmes for the first time. He came equipped with not just a rough idea for a collaborative effort but a detailed, eight-page prospectus of what the "learning outcomes"—module by module—should be and the best approach for delivering them. Providing further impetus to the project were two enthusiastic supporters: Archbishop John Myers of the Archdiocese of Newark and Bishop Arthur Serratelli of the Diocese of Paterson (who would be a speaker at our first-ever Pastor's Toolbox workshop).

Vital support came from two other outstanding leaders: Fr. Don Hummel of Newark's Office of Continuing Education of Priests and John Eriksen, then-superintendent of schools for the Diocese of Paterson. John was key in identifying faculty for the initial Toolbox for Pastoral Management. Others who provided valuable help along the way were Msgr. Jim Mahoney, vicar general in the Diocese of Paterson, and Kerry Robinson, executive director of the Leadership Roundtable, through her consistent advice and inspiration.

We're proud that the Toolbox for Pastoral Management is now an established program, offering multiple seminars annually at locations across the country. Reviews from attendees have been uniformly excellent, and an outside assessment by Dr. Vic Klimoski of St. John's University in Collegeville, Minnesota, was laudatory. But we're hardly resting on our laurels. We're committed to improving and fine-tuning the program to ensure it is consistent with the changing needs of new pastors, as well as the Catholic Church. The same can be said of this book. Regarding it as a dynamic project, we intend to add new chapters and revise existing ones in sync with the evolving Toolbox presentations.

Finally, I offer thanks to the people who have made this book possible. First and foremost are the individual members of our outstanding faculty who so skillfully presented their material at Toolbox sessions. A special callout is due to Geoff Boisi, founder of the National Leadership Roundtable on Church Management. Many thanks to Randy Young for his superior editorial skills in adapting these presentations to book format. He was able to capture our presenters' thoughts and, at the same time, honor their words. Thanks, too, to Kelly Tedesco, Lisa Metz, and Kimberly Mailley for their hard work in organizing the myriad details of the Toolbox events. And a very special thanks, once again, to Fr. Holmes for his outstanding work in orchestrating both the handbook and the workshop components of the Toolbox for Pastoral Management. He has proven to be a very gifted, and effective, maestro.

Introduction

Paul A. Holmes

Welcome to *A Pastor's Toolbox*!

It is no secret that Catholic pastors often feel overwhelmed and underprepared for the administrative rigors of their jobs. Today's parish leaders are expected to be holy and prayerful spiritual guides, great preachers, and compassionate confessors, and also to make important decisions in key areas like finance, budgeting, hiring and firing, fundraising, risk management, relationship-building, and more—often with virtually no transition or training. And with all the requisite education in philosophy and theology that seminaries must provide future pastors, in addition to all the needed formation in priestly spirituality and pastoral care, our seminaries can do little to prepare priests to deal with the difficult temporal issues pastors face.

A Pastor's Toolbox is designed to help fill that void. The chapters that follow contain valuable information, insights, and practical tools that pastors need in order to begin handling the complexities of parish management in the twenty-first century. Which budgeting and financial analysis competencies are key to running a strong fiscal house? What steps should your parish take to protect its assets? How do you manage the new skills essential to fundraising? Why is working seamlessly with laity so important to your long-term success? What do you need to know about hiring, evaluating, coaching, and inspiring members of your parish team? How do you deploy best practices to operate a parish effectively?

These questions and many more are candidly addressed in *A Pastor's Toolbox* by experts, both clergy and lay, with years of experience and leadership in their respective fields. With a generous grant from Lilly Endowment, both Seton Hall University and the National Leadership

Roundtable on Church Management have collaborated in creating a weeklong face-to-face workshop experience to address the critical issues of parish management—especially for new pastors. Offered over the last several years in various locations across the country, these fifteen presentations are now reaching a much wider audience, thanks to Liturgical Press who has published the handbook you now hold.

A Pastor's Toolbox begins with "A Theology of Management: Why We Do What We Do," in which Fr. Paul Holmes sets forth the spiritual reasons for understanding the pastor's administrative tasks as flowing from (and not antithetical to) his baptismal and ordained identity as priest, prophet, and king (essay 1). You will also read Fr. Robert Stagg's view of a pastor's power and authority in "Pastoral Leadership" (essay 2), noting that a pastor's power comes from above and below, but just as important, from within. Jim Lundholm-Eades provides a handy roadmap for a pastor's first months in his "Six-Month Game Plan," identifying the "sanctifying" role as a necessary focus when starting out (essay 3). In addition, a new pastor must look to the day-to-day operations of his parish, so Maria Mendoza helps the pastor hit the ground running in her "Getting Started: The Parish Business Office" (essay 4).

Today's parish leader does more than celebrate the sacraments, crucial as this is; he must also manage the parish's human, financial, and physical resources. Fr. David Boettner writes of how to deftly manage employees and volunteers in "Developing a Comprehensive Human Resources Program" (essay 5), and John McGovern provides the details of "Risk Management" (essay 6), insisting that a pastor cannot eliminate risks to people, money, and physical plant, but he can surely minimize those risks and keep them from spinning out of control. In his "Best Practices in Parish Internal Financial Controls," Charles Zech asserts that, while the Catholic Church is not a business, pastors do have a stewardship responsibility to employ sound business practices and tools (essay 7). And in "Fundraising as Christian Stewardship" (essay 8), Kerry Robinson describes the major obstacles that have traditionally stood in the way of effective fundraising within the church, and how infusing the task with "a palpable sense of joy, purpose, and an incredible closeness to God" can help overcome these roadblocks.

None of a pastor's administrative tasks can be accomplished by him alone. Mission-driven institutions like the church require that the pastor find ways to partner with various people, both in and beyond the parish's borders, inviting them to become part of the church's mission. To this end, Fr. Jack Wall demonstrates how to "partner with excellence" in "Pastoring and Administering a Mission-Driven Church" (essay 9). And in essay 10, Dennis Corcoran offers sage advice about the critical role of building parish and finance councils to assist the pastor in his management of the parish. Michael Brough, in "Standards for Excellence" (essay 11), explains that there are processes, policies, and structures to help pastors stay on course, presenting a collection of performance benchmarks that offer a comprehensive blueprint for a well-managed and responsibly run Catholic parish.

One of a priest's chief tasks as pastor is pastoral planning, so Jim Lundholm-Eades provides some important tools in "Parish Planning" (essay 12). The pastor must also be savvy in handling the diverse nature of today's parish, so Arturo Chávez provides some very helpful reminders in "Unity in Diversity" (essay 13). A ready resource exists for all pastors and Msgr. Franklyn Casale talks about making good use of them in "The Pastor and the Diocese" (essay 14). And, finally, all pastors, both those with little or no experience and those with a great deal, must attend to all these tasks, both spiritual and administrative, without losing sight of their own health. Fr. Paul Manning, in "In Pursuit of Priestly Well-Being" (essay 15), looks at the church's ordination rite and finds indications of how to remain healthy in both mind and body.

There are, of course, many more issues facing pastors in today's church. It is nevertheless the hope of all those who have collaborated to make *A Pastor's Toolbox* a reality that this handbook will assist in making the pastorate a grace-filled and successful endeavor, full of blessings for the pastor himself but also for all those committed to his pastoral care!

A Theology of Management:
Why We Do What We Do

Paul A. Holmes

In giving new pastors the skills and know-how they need to handle the complexities of church management in the twenty-first century, *A Pastor's Toolbox* is by necessity focused on what a pastor does. Here at the beginning of this handbook, I'd like to shift that natural focus to *why* a pastor does what he does. Put another way, I'd like to concentrate on a theology of management.

I believe, quite simply, there is only one goal in your work as a pastor: the *salus animarum*—the salvation of souls that was begun by Jesus Christ and continues through his church. This salvation takes several forms.

First, there is *your* salvation. You're one of those souls in the *salus animarum*. From a theological and spiritual point of view, you will be a pastor—a shepherd—of many souls, including your own.

Second, there is the salvation of your sisters and brothers—the ones who have been entrusted to your care. There is your management team, the liturgical assembly that gathers each day (especially on Sundays), and, beyond them, all your registered parishioners. And canon law asks pastors not to forget what I refer to as your "yet-to-be-registered" parishioners. In fact, canon law directs pastors "to make every effort, even with the collaboration of the Christian faithful, so that the message of the gospel comes also to those who have ceased the practice of their religion or do not profess the true faith" (c. 528 §1).

So, What Are We Managing?

The fact that we're even discussing a "theology of management" might surprise a lot of people. It would have especially surprised many bishops over a half-century ago. One particular American bishop wrote in 1948, "I observe that some pastors have arbitrarily and boldly presumed to charge the parish treasury large amounts of money paid to a lay parish secretary. This is definitely unlawful and cannot be tolerated. All secretarial work must be done by the pastors and their assistants."[1]

How the world—and the church—has changed! But even in a more modern context, what exactly are we hoping to manage in our roles as pastors? The answer, I believe, has three parts.

First, you will be managing *resources*. These include *human resources*, namely the time and talents of people; *material resources*, particularly your physical surroundings, also known as the "plant"; and *spiritual resources*, essentially the hopes and dreams of the people in your care.

Second, you will be managing *expectations*. This includes wrestling with weighty theological questions such as where are we coming from, where are we going to, and how are we going to get there.

And finally, you will be managing *risks*, for if we don't manage risks today, we'll be managing crises tomorrow.

Recognizing the Roles of a Pastor

Vital to an understanding of a theology of management, I think, is a recognition of what exactly the roles, duties, and tasks of a pastor are. And I can assure you there is more than a nuance of difference among each.

The Six Priestly Roles

In *The Handbook of Religion and Social Institutions*, Dean Hoge writes that as far back as the 1950s research focused on the six roles that priests play or inhabit: (1) teacher, (2) preacher, (3) priest, (4) pastor, (5) administrator, and (6) organizer.[2]

It's clear that any discussion about a theology of management must take into account all six roles if we are to honestly answer the question, "Why do we do what we do?" From a scriptural point of view, I think we can generally acknowledge that Jesus not only inhabited all six roles, he *modeled* them for us. Consider:

His disciples actually called him *Teacher*, and he himself told them, "You call me Teacher and Lord—and you are right, for that is what I am" (John 13:13).

Jesus was also the *preacher* par excellence, as evidenced by what he said immediately after visiting the synagogue, opening the scroll of Isaiah, and proclaiming his first (and I'd say only) liturgical homily: "Today this scripture has been fulfilled in your hearing" (Luke 4:21). In this, he was telling the assembly that salvation was happening before their very eyes—or, more appropriately, with their very ears.

If he wasn't before, Jesus certainly was a *priest* on the Cross, offering the sacrifice of his body and blood as we do today in his memory. And, as one of the Prefaces of Easter declares, he was what we can never be: He "showed himself [to be] the Priest, the Altar, and the Lamb of sacrifice." Once again, he was the priest without equal.

Was he also a *pastor?* Of course he was. The Latin word *pastor* means shepherd, and we remember that he called himself the Good Shepherd. No finer pastor ever lived as he sought out the lost sheep and carried it home. In fact, one of the earliest images of Christ is a sculpture showing a young shepherd (pastor) carrying a lamb on his shoulders. In art and in the hearts of the earliest Christians, Jesus was a pastor (shepherd) before he was anything else.

As for the roles of *administrator* and *organizer,* St. Paul included administrator (and, I would guess, organizer) in a whole list of ministries within the church in his first letter to the Corinthians:

> Now concerning spiritual gifts, brothers and sisters, I do not want you to be uninformed. . . . Now there are varieties of gifts, but the same Spirit. . . . And God has appointed in the church first apostles, second prophets, third teachers, then deeds of power, then gifts of healings, forms of assistance, *forms of leadership,* various kinds of tongues. (1 Cor 12:1, 4, 28, italics added)

Paul stops counting spiritual gifts long before he gets to the gift of administration, seeming to throw it in at the end. But this is not to discount administration as a gift of the Spirit, or to deny that it is an "appointment" in much the same way that apostles, prophets, and teachers are appointed. Miracles are in the mix, but as you'll discover, you will be expected as pastor to perform quite a number of these!

How Many Hats Does a Pastor Wear?

Taking those six basic roles into account, what, then, would a job description of "Catholic priest" look like?

It is an interesting question—one which the authors Joseph Ippolito, Mark Latcovich, and Joyce Malyn-Smith expended a good deal of time trying to answer. As part of an assessment project they called *In Fulfillment of Their Mission: The Duties and Tasks of a Roman Catholic Priest*, they developed this simple description: "A Catholic Priest [serves] the people primarily in parishes, and also in schools, hospitals, prisons, and other settings, through acts of Christian Ministry including celebrating liturgy and sacraments, education, *administration* [my emphasis] and pastoral care."[3] From that baseline they developed a list of nine duties that a priest is expected to perform today as integral parts of his job: (1) he celebrates liturgy and sacraments, (2) he provides pastoral care and spiritual guidance, (3) he teaches the faith, (4) *he leads parish administration* [again, my emphasis], (5) he practices a ministry of presence with parish groups, (6) he participates in the life of the diocesan church, (7) he engages with diverse publics, (8) he engages in professional development, and (9) he engages in personal development.

Unfortunately, the priest does not get to pick and choose which of these nine duties he will perform. We are expected to perform *all* of them. It is the fourth duty, however, that I'd like to single out. When you lead the administration of a parish, you are fulfilling a major responsibility in your life as a priest and pastor. Be aware that it is not an extra duty. *It is at the core of who you are.*

To add another layer to the already complex job of being a pastor, the aforementioned assessment project found there are five essential tasks that help define the duty of "leading parish administration":

1. Initiating strategic planning grounded in Gospel values and diocesan mission.
2. Overseeing the implementation of a strategic plan.
3. Leading the parish's pastoral and finance councils.
4. Animating ministries, apostolates, and volunteers of the parish.
5. Overseeing the stewardship of parish finances, including budget, fundraising, and diocesan assessment.[4]

The Practices of Ministry

The duties and tasks I've just described could collectively be called the "practices of ministry." They are important to know because they will consume the bulk of your time and energy as pastor. In *Introducing the Practice of Ministry* Kathleen Cahalan provides a theological basis for what we do as pastors. More specifically, she explains that ministry is but one vocation among many in the Christian community and is best identified through the practices of teaching, preaching, leading worship and prayer, pastoral care, social ministry, and administration.

Ministry is a verb, Cahalan affirms, something that people *do*. And she emphasizes that ministry is learned over time and through great practice. "The professional practice of ministry constitutes the dynamic interaction of what we know, competence in the skill to act, and the moral virtues of the person we are and are becoming," she writes. "Practice is the integration of doing, knowing, and being."[5]

Finally, she reminds us that God practices divine communion as three Persons in relationship. As "Trinity," God is a communion of divine relationality who made us for both relationship and communion. As such, the practices of God are meant to draw us into deeper communion with one another and the three divine Persons.

For its part, the Trinity conveys an insight that is immensely important to our ministry. All of us have been created in the image and likeness of a God who isn't only singular (God is one), but plural (God is three) as well. In other words, God doesn't have to go outside himself for intimacy, nor does he have to go beyond himself to find partners in his work.

Some students recently took a course titled "The Theology and Practice of Pastoral Ministry" as part of a Lilly Endowment grant. The students discussed the benefits of having pastors write sermons in community. What emerged from their colloquy is important to our own discussion. "It dawned upon us," the course leader recalls, "that perhaps one of the radical implications of the Trinity, the divine community that is God, is that pastors should never do anything alone, that all ministry should be done in community."[6]

I would suggest that one of the major implications of a "theology of management" is that none of us should be acting like a "lone ranger," or a Zeus sitting atop Mount Olympus hurling lightning bolts and issuing divine fiats. As singular creatures made in the image of a "plural" God, we have a theological mandate to go beyond ourselves and act in community. Indeed, all ministry should be done in community.

The Pastor as Priest, Prophet, and King

Perhaps the most theological way to understand a pastor's ministry is to remind ourselves of our baptismal identity. Ever since our baptism, we have not only been priests but prophets and kings as well. Our ordination to priesthood only served to strengthen those three faces—known collectively as the *munera Christi*—just as Christ was priest, prophet, and king.

The documents of the Second Vatican Council never tire of speaking of this tripartite identity. In *Lumen Gentium* and the decrees on bishops and the training of priests, as well as the decree on the laity, our identity as priests, prophets, and kings is continually highlighted. The Catechism picked up on this: "By ordination one is enabled to act as a representative of Christ, Head of the Church, in his triple office of priest, prophet, and king" (§1581).

As the *munera Christi* make up our identity, so do they comprise our job description and work agenda. Let's take a closer look at what I mean by that.

What is essential about our identity as priests?

After only two years in my first parish, I was invited to join the staff of the Newark (New Jersey) Cathedral of the Sacred Heart, the most perfect expression of the French Gothic in the Western Hemisphere. Only the stained-glass windows at Chartres are brighter. Over the years, I came to enjoy giving tours of this most magnificent building. One of the things I recall as I spoke about the stunningly beautiful colors streaming in from those stained-glass windows was the story of a seven-year-old girl who was taking the tour of another famous church. She listened carefully to the stories of the saints pictured in the windows and, at the end of the tour, announced to her mother that she knew who the saints were. "So, who are they?" the mother asked. "They're the ones who let the light shine through," the wise young girl replied.

This, of course, is just what priests are supposed to do. Even the word saint in Latin is *sanctus*—the word for holy. We're the ones who, in our *munus sanctificandi,* make things holy. And in doing so, especially as pastors, we are supposed to become saints; we are supposed to endeavor to make all things, and all people, holy. That little girl I just mentioned got it just right: we're the ones who let the light—the light of Christ—shine through all we are and all we do.

What is essential about our identity as prophets?

Most of the theology written about the *munus propheticum* focuses on our role as preachers and teachers. But I would like to sharpen that focus a bit. To do that, I need to tell you what I know about sheep. Yes, sheep.

I was born in Newark, New Jersey, and I can assure you there weren't many sheep in my neighborhood. There wasn't even much grass. All I know about sheep I learned years later from the window washer at the North American College in Rome. His name was Achille. After noticing that he'd disappear for weeks at a time, Achille finally told me one day that he wasn't really a window washer. He was a shepherd, and he'd save up all his vacation days and take them all at once so he could return to the Abruzzi hills every few months to tend his sheep.

It turns out that everything we've heard about sheep from Jesus is true. As a shepherd, Achille would go out into the countryside and call his sheep—by their individual names—and each would come running at the sound of his voice. Achille confirmed for me a truth about sheep that underlies one of Jesus' parables. He told me that sheep hate being alone. In fact, should a lamb get separated from the flock, it will start shaking from fear, eating only the grass that grows at its feet. But once those blades of grass are gone, the sheep won't take one more step to eat, or even drink from a pool if one was nearby. It will shiver and shake—to death.

That's why Jesus insisted that a shepherd has to leave the other ninety-nine of his flock and go find the one that is lost. A good shepherd knows that a sheep on its own is a matter of life and death. This is why I think it's important to remember that the *munus docendi* may be about teaching and preaching, but it's also about *reaching.*

Indeed, reaching is what we're supposed to do through our own teaching and preaching. We're supposed to reach those who are listening to us—and more than that—we need to reach those who aren't sitting before us too (those "yet-to-be-registered" parishioners).

What is essential about our identity as kings?

When speaking about the *munus regendi*, it is common to speak about governance (in fact, this task of Christ is often called the *munus gubernandi*). As pastor, the governance of the parish is entrusted to your care. This requires pastors to be familiar with an astonishing range of issues, including financial, human resources, risk management, physical plant, and diversity, to name just a few.

Any theology of management today is well grounded in these tasks of governance. But I'd like to focus on another dimension of the *munus regendi*, and do so with a story.

One of my favorite works of art is Rodin's *Burghers of Calais*, a larger-than-life-size sculpture of six men in ropes and chains with disbelief, horror, and fear written on their faces. There is some fascinating history behind this iconic work of art. When England's Edward III laid siege to Calais in 1347, France's King Philip VI ordered the city to resist. The people of Calais—every man, woman, and child—fought valiantly, even to the point of starvation. And when they were finally forced to surrender, Edward was so angry that he wanted the city razed to the ground. After his privy council intervened, however, he offered to spare the city's residents if six members of Calais' town council agreed to die in their place. It was this moment—when these six defeated men appeared, with nooses around their necks—that Rodin captured in his famous sculpture.

What we don't learn from looking at the iconic work of art is that the burghers' lives were spared. England's Queen Philippa is alleged to have begged for their release, saying to her husband, "If not for love of me or our unborn child, then, please, for the love of Christ, let these men go!"

This immortal story hints at the power of kings. They can do what so few are able to do: they can grant clemency; they can let the guilty go free; they can forgive the unforgiveable. This, I feel, is the essence of the *munus regendi*—the virtue of unmitigated mercy. Why is this so important to our discussion? Because as you go about your pastoral ministry, this is the virtue that will speak the loudest about your role as king. As a pastor, you will be charged with managing—but managing in a way that flows from your baptismal and ordained identity.

Authenticity and the Munera Christi

What does your baptismal and ordained identity say about your managing ability? Above all, I'm suggesting that you must be authentic. In other words, you have to be *who* you are *wherever* you are. Let me put that in the context of priest, prophet, king—with an emphasis on six skills that will come in handy as you go about your tasks of pastoral management, viz., a priest's holiness and gratitude; a prophet's truthfulness and fidelity; and a king's forgiveness and judgment.

Priest as manager: The symbolic locus of the priest is, of course, the altar. The person your parishioners see at the altar each day must be the same individual they meet everywhere else—over in the school, at the parish finance council, in the pastor's office. The skills (or virtues) you hone at that altar are, especially, holiness and gratitude. And applying those two skills to the five management tasks you have as pastor might look like this:

Holiness

1. Ensure that elements of strategic plan let the Light of Christ shine through.
2. Ensure that prayerfulness guides the plan's implementation.
3. Guide parish and finance council members in holiness.
4. Lead ministers and volunteers toward holiness.
5. Ensure stewardship efforts are grounded in ethical principles.

Gratitude

1. Ensure that strategic plan has a eucharistic focus.
2. Ensure that implementation expresses gratitude for everyone's gifts.
3. Express gratitude for the work of parish councils.
4. Keep all ministers and volunteers grateful for their ministry.
5. Express gratitude to contributors and donors.

Prophet as manager: The symbolic locus of the prophet is the pulpit. Authenticity requires that the person you are in the pulpit must be the same individual your parishioners meet everywhere else. If we admit that the skills you hone in that pulpit are, especially, truthfulness and fidelity to the Gospel, then applying those two skills to the five management tasks you have as pastor might look like this:

Truthfulness

1. Be honest about the parish's ability to reach strategic goals.
2. Keep planning participants grounded in the truth of the Gospel.
3. Guide councils in truthful reporting in both programs and finances.
4. Support all ministers in an honest appraisal of their skills and talents.
5. Ensure that the parish budget reflects mission and goals, and vice versa.

Fidelity

1. Ensure that the strategic plan is faithful to Catholic teaching.
2. Encourage planning participants to deepen their faith.
3. Ensure that council agendas are faithful to parish mission.
4. Animate all ministers and volunteers in faithfulness to church and Gospel.
5. Reach out to donors and contributors with an emphasis on Gospel fidelity.

King as manager: Acquainted as we are with the story of Rodin's *Burghers of Calais*, we can affirm that the symbolic locus of the king is the confessional. The man in the confessional must be the same man your parishioners meet everywhere else. The skills that are honed in the confessional are, especially, forgiveness and judgment. And, if so, then applying the two skills (or virtues) of the confessional would look like this:

Forgiveness

1. Ensure openness, by all, to the parish plan.
2. In overseeing implementation, be patient with all participants.

3. Guide councils' openness to all council members' gifts.

4. Gently ensure that all parish ministers and volunteers have requisite skills.

5. Cultivate donors' and contributors' responsible stewardship of the parish.

Judgment

1. Exercise careful judgment about when to initiate the planning process.

2. Be careful that goals include care for the financially and spiritually poor.

3. Ensure parish's councils have proper membership and no conflicts of interest.

4. Offer ongoing formation for sacramental and program ministers.

5. Ensure that contributors and donors are mindful of Gospel values.

In sum, the virtues of holiness and gratitude, of truthfulness and fidelity, of forgiveness and judgment, are the same skills on which a strong theology of pastoral management focuses our attention.

Is the Parish a Factory, Family, Jungle, or Culture?

Two experts in organizational theory, Leo Bolman and Terrence Deal, suggest that we can view our parishes in one of four different ways: as a factory, a family, a jungle, or a culture.[7] You might think that none of these adequately describes what a parish really is (except, perhaps, a family), but you need to be aware that you and the people you will be working with will unconsciously view the parish in one, or more, of these ways.

Parish as Factory

If you, your staff, or your parishioners view the parish as similar to a *factory*, you are said to be viewing it through a *structural frame*. This view emphasizes the parish's goals, specialized roles, and formal relationships. The structures of the parish are designed to fit its environment, and there must be a clear division of labor, rules, policies, procedures, and hierarchies. The most benign understanding of the structural frame is simple: the goal is to find a way to organize and structure groups and teams in order to get results.

Pastor's challenge: You need to find a way to attune structure to Gospel, mission, and goals.

Strategy for change: You may need to consider realigning formal roles and relationships.

But before you consider making any changes in parish structure, Bolman and Deal caution that change in any organization can (1) cause people to feel incompetent, needy, and powerless, (2) create confusion and unpredictability, (3) generate conflict, and (4) create loss.

Parish as Family

If you view the parish as a *family*, you are said to be viewing it through a *human resources frame.* Your parish is like an extended family, with individual needs, feelings, prejudices, skills, and limitations. Therefore, the human resources frame focuses on how to tailor the parish to satisfy human (and spiritual) needs, and to build positive and interpersonal and group dynamics.

Pastor's challenge: You will need to align organizational and spiritual needs.

Strategy for change: Focus on training and support for your parish management team, as well as for all those collaborating with you in ministry.

Parish as Jungle

If you view the parish as a *jungle*, you are said to be viewing it through a *political frame*. From this perspective, the parish serves as an arena, or contest, where different interests compete for scarce resources. And not unlike the U.S. Congress, a lot of time is spent bargaining, negotiating, compromising, and even coercing. The political frame focuses on how to cope with power and conflict, build coalitions, hone political skills, and deal with internal and external politics.

Pastor's challenge: You need to develop an agenda and get everyone to sign on to it.

Strategy for change: Establish various "arenas" for decision making.

Parish as Culture

If you view the parish as a *culture*, you are said to be viewing it through a *symbolic frame*. I happen to favor this frame, since it seems best suited for what we are called upon to do as priests. The symbolic frame treats the parish as a theater or, as Bolman and Deal call it, a "temple." This culture is created and propelled by rituals, ceremonies, stories, heroes and myths, and not necessarily by policies and formal authority. The symbolic frame focuses on how to shape a culture that gives purpose and meaning to work and build team spirit through ritual, ceremony, and story.

Pastor's challenge: You need to create (or, at least, protect and embody) faith, beauty, and meaning.

Strategy for change: Remember transition rituals.

Bolman and Deal maintain that a successful organization must develop all four frames. While we may personally feel comfortable in only one of them, the ability to recognize with what frames your team members and parishioners are in sync will be an important measure of your success as a pastor.

A Final Thought

I've focused heavily on your baptismal and ordained identities to explain how the pivotal roles of priest, prophet, and king can inform your actions as a pastor. The three symbolic locations attached to these roles—altar, pulpit, and confessional—are all familiar to us, and the people around us come to expect that we're being authentic when they meet us at these venues.

I firmly believe that the skills and virtues we bring to each of these locations are the same ones that should guide our work as pastors. For that reason, I urge you to keep the roles of priest, prophet, and king uppermost in mind as you learn about and become acclimated to your myriad responsibilities as pastor. Never lose sight of the fact that:

Holiness and gratitude need to be staples of your pastoral demeanor.

Truthfulness and fidelity will be two important measures of your success.

And, finally, forgiveness and judgment will serve as the cornerstones of your management style.

Rest assured that if you abide by these tenets, you will not only act as though you know *what* you're doing as you go about the *salus animarum*, but you will also be acting in a way that suggests you know *why* you're doing it. More than anything, that is what a theology of management should accomplish.

Endnotes

1. Pittsburgh Bishop Hugh Boyle, qtd. in Kristen Hannum, "The Parish That Works: Business Practices for the Church," *U.S. Catholic* 76, No. 7 (July 2011): 12–13.

2. Dean R. Hoge, "Religious Leadership/Clergy," in *The Handbook of Religion and Social Institutions*, edited by Helen Rose Ebaugh (New York: Springer Science+Business Media, Inc., 2006), 373.

3. Joseph Ippolito, Mark Latcovich, and Joyce Malyn-Smith, *In Fulfillment of Their Mission: The Duties and Tasks of a Roman Catholic Priest* (Washington, DC: National Catholic Educational Association, 2008), 8.

4. Ibid., 16.

5. Kathleen Cahalan, *Introducing the Practice of Ministry* (Collegeville, MN: Liturgical Press, 2010), xi.

6. Qtd. in Christian Reformed Church in North America, "Creating a Culture of Pastoral Excellence," Sustaining Pastoral Excellence Project Report, 2007. See http://www2.crcna.org/site_uploads/uploads/spe/lillyannualreport_2006.pdf, 8.

7. See Lee G. Bolman and Terrence E. Deal, *Reframing Organizations: Artistry, Choice, and Leadership*, 4th ed. (San Francisco: Jossey Bass, 2008), 15–16.

2

Pastoral Leadership

Robert Stagg

I'd like to share with you my candid thoughts on what it's like to be a pastor today—the joys as well as the challenges. Clearly, the enterprise we're about is one of the toughest jobs on earth. It's also one of the best. You walk into a new assignment one day, go up to the pulpit, turn on the pulpit lights, and realize that the stakes have never been higher. It's never been harder to be a pastor than it is today. Pastors are on the firing line. A challenge to be sure—but an exciting one.

Let me try to describe it with an example. Recently, I was driving down New Jersey's Garden State Parkway, and I stopped at the home of one of my sisters. In her backyard, I found my niece playing with a couple of kids, and nearby was a picnic table with a turtle sitting right on top of it. I asked, "Who put the turtle there?" And my niece Liz responded, "It just got there."

We all know a turtle just doesn't get on top of a table unless somebody puts it there.

While it's a pretty unflattering analogy, you and I are kind of like that turtle: we've been put in a lot of places in our lives. As for me, I've landed in many neat places—most of them none of my doing. What comes foremost to mind is my first pastorate, which came about sixteen years out and is probably the most exciting thing that ever happened to me. I was thrilled to be a deacon, thrilled to be newly ordained. I prayed for my first pastorate and was ecstatic when it came. But once I got there, I felt a weight, a responsibility. I realized the spiritual care of these souls was being placed in my hands.

Just like the turtle sitting on the picnic table, I've had an awful lot of help and support along the way. And it's really useful to turn around to see how we got to where we are.

Watching and Learning

In my case, I was a director of campus ministry when I was named pastor for the first time. Vince Dwyer, who ran the "ministry to priest" program for many years and was a mentor of mine, had me moving around the country, as well as to Canada and England, giving priests' retreats. I was having a lot of fun as a campus minister when my archbishop at the time—now Cardinal Theodore McCarrick—called to say he wanted me to go to this particular suburban parish. When I was named, I called two pastors who I knew were doing really good work and asked them, "Do you mind if I come to your parish and spend a couple of days with you and your staff?" They said, "Come," and so I spent three days tailing these really good pastors, listening to their staffs, talking to the pastoral associates, and sitting in on staff meetings. And I knew right away they were artful in what they did, that they were doing very impressive stuff. And in many cases, it was unknown to the rest of the diocese.

That grounding was really helpful because as I've since learned, you get a clean slate when you go into many parishes. The place [then] Archbishop McCarrick sent me to was truly a *tabula rasa* ("blank slate"). And that's a good thing—you have a clear field ahead of you. It allows you to dream your dream and adopt your pastoral model. You have to be wary, though, of attempting everything right away. There was a man, for example, I wanted to name as business administrator my first week as pastor. I wrestled with doing so and realized I probably needed to get a better sense of the impact of that decision before making it. You come to recognize that sometimes the best decisions are the ones you *don't* make.

The parish I'm in now, the Church of the Presentation Parish in Upper Saddle River, New Jersey, has a staff of twenty-five, not including a school that we cosponsor, compared to a staff of six in my first parish. It's one of the largest parishes in the state, and that requires a lot of supervision and a lot of coaching.

I'd like to tell you a little bit about the pastoral model we have in place there, which is a very active one. We run ten annual parish retreats, a number of them on-site. We also have a medical mission in Haiti where we send about thirty people, mostly doctors and nurses, twice a year. We just bought a piece of property in Haiti and are building a clinic. We're also in New Orleans about five times a year with groups of between twenty and sixty people per trip, and we send our youth to Mexico and Costa Rica each summer to build homes and teach English. In addition to that, we run three weekly soup kitchens and have within our parish sixty small Christian communities—SCCs—which are part of the renewal experience for their members. More about these in a little bit.

Keep the Momentum Going

So, there's a lot going on, and it started long before I got there. My job as pastor, in a sense, is to keep the momentum going. And, as I've found, that involves a different kind of pressure. It reminds me of a skit I saw on *The Ed Sullivan Show*, which I watched on TV with my family as a kid. They used to have a fellow perform who was great at spinning plates on top of long poles. He'd get a plate going, then walk over to a second pole and get it going, and a third—and by then, of course, he'd have to run back to the first plate to keep it spinning, then to the second, and so on. Does that sound like a familiar exercise to all of you? You have people from your last parish calling and saying, "Can you join me for dinner?" You've now got a finance council for the first time, you're sitting on a diocesan board, and you're trying to develop a staff. You have a lot of plates spinning around.

The other image I have is of bicycling. When you ride a bike, you need a good sense of balance. You can't be too rigid or too relaxed. Either way, you're going to get into trouble. The same principle applies to being a pastoral minister. You really need a keen sense of balance. While you need to look at all the things you can possibly do—we're generalists, after all—concentrating on too much of any one thing can get you into trouble. It can cause you to sway and maybe even fall off the bike. A good stabilizing force for leading a long, fruitful life as a pastor, given all the demands it imposes, is to have a sense of humor.

Another helpful piece of advice is this: take advantage of the fresh set of eyes you have when you first enter a parish. You're only going to have them for a little while. A friend of mine was named to a new parish and decided to show up three weeks before he was supposed to. But he didn't tell anyone. He just put on his golf shirt and slacks, drove the forty miles to the parish, walked into the church, and stayed for the liturgy. No one knew he was there. Well, at his first parish council meeting after taking over as pastor, he listened to members praise to the heavens the hospitality, the singing, the way everyone was welcomed into the eucharistic community. At this point, he piped up and said, "Let me stop you right there. I came here about a month ago, and there were no signs to tell me which one of the buildings here was the church. Once inside, there was no one to greet me. We started singing, and I had no idea which page to turn to in the hymnal. To the contrary, I didn't get the impression the church was particularly warm, inviting *or* hospitable."

And that actually wasn't a bad thing for him to say because it set a marker down for far-reaching improvements, which he immediately undertook with the full support of his pastoral council. He acted while he had a fresh set of eyes.

When it comes to being an effective pastoral leader, I believe there are three overarching responsibilities we all have: One is to be keeper of the vision; two, selecting a staff; and three, assessing the needs of the parish.

Keeper of the Vision

Let me first address the role of keeper of the vision. I like to sail and have frequently sailed in the waters off the Jersey Shore. Unlike a motorboat, sailboats require a captain who has to know which way the wind is blowing, what the tide is doing, where the currents are running. You have to have all your feelers out. And with your hand firmly on the tiller, you can make your sailboat go in the direction you choose. The job of the pastor, as I see it, is to be the guy at the tiller. When you set out, you have to have an end in sight. In other words, what's my pastoral plan? In what direction do I want to lead this parish?

Clearly, the biggest factor in any parish is the pastor. There can be good pastors, and there can be bad pastors. There can be state-of-the-art pastors, and there can be old-school pastors. Regardless, you're the focal point, the link with the diocese, the representative of the institutional church and the parish. As the keeper of the vision, you must set sail with the end in sight.

There was a swimmer years ago by the name of Florence Chadwick who was swimming the English Channel between England and France. It was her first attempt at the twenty-mile distance, and she swam all day and all night, never losing sight of the lights along the Cliffs of Dover at night. Then the mists came up, and Chadwick suddenly stopped swimming, only about a mile from her destination along the cliffs. She yelled at her handlers, who were alongside her in boats, "Get me out of the water!" And they yelled back, "Florence, you're almost there! Finish the swim!" And she shot back, "No. You have to take me out, immediately!" Later on, there was a small press conference, and Chadwick was asked, "Were there sharks?" "Were you cold?" "Were you cramping?" And she answered, "No," to each. "The mist came in, and I couldn't see the lights along the cliffs any more. I lost all perspective, and I couldn't stand it."

The pastor's job is to keep that perspective. You have to set out with the end in sight and ask yourself if what you're doing will take you in the direction you need to go. Oftentimes, our vision can get pretty cloudy with all the things that crop up daily. I'm sure you know what I mean: you take a day off and when you return there are a hundred e-mails and twenty-five voice messages waiting for you. Sometimes you'll go a week without ever seeing the end in sight. The good news, however, is that there is a solution, and it starts with better planning and having competent people around you—people to whom you can delegate responsibilities. If you have an able assistant, for example, who can wade through those hundred e-mails and take them down to a handful of meaningful ones deserving your attention, then you'll have time to focus on those things that really matter to you as pastor. You'll be able to keep your perspective.

The Sources of Pastoral Power

I see pastoral power as a three-legged stool. We have power from above. There's the bishop who laid his hands on our heads, conferred what we call legitimate authority from above, and he then sent us forth to serve. Then there's power that we draw from below, from our congregations. It's the "street cred" we get from the people. And finally, there's the pastoral power that emanates from within *us*. It feeds on our gifts, our talents, our passion. You could call it the fire in our belly.

More important, you have to have all three legs for the stool to function. If there are only two legs, we won't be effective. A good example of that is the sexual abuse crisis that surfaced in 2002. The bishops had a lot of power at the time from above, but they lost their "street cred." People jumped ship and refused to follow the bishops. The bishops only had two of the three essential powers.

Another example are the men who were ordained with us but who have since left the ministry—many to get married. They no longer have legitimate authority. They're missing that critical leg.

And then there are some of our colleagues who have the legitimate authority, but they lack the fire in their belly. They've run out of gas and often don't want to be a pastor anymore. They want to spend the next fifteen years before retirement just chillin'. Unfortunately, these individuals often fail to unlock the incredible potential of their congregations—the "street cred" part.

So, I hope the message is clear: if you've got all three legs of the stool, you've either achieved, or are well on your way to achieving, effective pastoral leadership. Just as importantly, pastoral vision—being able to see and work effectively toward a definable end—can put that leadership goal within your grasp. The pastor's job, clearly, is to be able to connect the dots.

Pastoral councils can help you sustain that vision. They are essentially the board of trustees for the parish, focused on questions such as "Where are we going?" "What needs to be done?" "What's our overarching principle?" The councils' vision really impacts our own. When Vatican II came along and launched these pastoral councils, they also set forth a four-point model for them: word, worship, community building, and service. The "Big Four" has been drilled into each of us, and we've done adaptations of that model for years. But along came a fellow from Minnesota, Bill Huebsch, who wrote a terrific little book called *Dreams and Visions*, in which he asks the questions, "If the Big Four is everybody's pastoral model, then why aren't we firing people up? Why is there no impact?" And even more importantly, "How do you go from a good parish to a great parish?"[1]

The Challenge of Being Catholic

Huebsch points out that many people just aren't enthusiastic about their faith. They're just meeting the minimum requirements to get a baby baptized or to use the church for a wedding. They drop the kids off at church, go shopping, then pick them up. "Drop and shop," we call it. They have a lukewarm response to the Mass: they don't sing out with a full voice, if they sing at all, and mutter their responses. Mass attendance is low. Indeed, a Gallop Poll showed that in 1960 Mass attendance was 74 percent of parishioners. It fell to 40 percent in 2003, and according to the church's own polls is even lower. Anecdotal feedback suggests that as many as 60 to 70 percent of parents with a child in religious education or Catholic school are not themselves actively taking part in weekly Mass or other activities as part of parish life.

Other disturbing signs are the fact that collections are down, and that Catholics give at a very low rate compared to other Christian denominations. It's also hard to get volunteers—sometimes just to meet the needs of current programs. And adult members of the parish don't show up for faith formation groups or offerings, even when those offerings are fabulous and well-planned. People don't seem interested. There's just no fire in the belly of the parish.

No wonder the job of pastor has become such a challenge. It requires us to constantly review—and revise—our pastoral model. In his wonderful book, Bill Huebsch adds two more pillars to the Big Four pastoral model handed down by Vatican II. One of those is parish retreats, or group encounters, and the second is adult faith-sharing groups, or small Christian communities.

At my parish, we have a long history of involvement in all six of these areas. And that's really what the job of pastor is—melding all the pieces of this model together. Most people in our parish, for example, go through what we call a "cornerstone experience." That's a twenty-six-hour retreat for men and women, separately. They show up at six o'clock Friday evening and leave at eight o'clock Saturday evening. We've been doing it for thirty-one years and have helped set up similar programs in twenty other states around the country. The biggest challenge for me each year is to draw as many new moms and dads into the program as possible. What goes on at these sessions? Well, there's a lot of sharing of faith and a lot of sharing of personal stories—all designed to shed light on questions such as "What is God's plan for me?" "How does the Bible affect me?" "What does it mean to be a Christian today?"

What we're creating through these "cornerstone" retreats is a sacrament of community, where the follow-up is much more important than the event itself. People are introduced to one another, and they form these small Christian communities that meet weekly, biweekly, or monthly. Sometimes they meet as couples. We have about sixty-five of these communities that are very active in our parish. As they meet, they may "break open," or reflect upon, the Word as it applies to their lives or perhaps entertain a "question of the week." These people are looking to get involved, and we need to continue to open up new opportunities for them to do this—which, in turn, creates more ministries and outreach.

Fixing Outdated Church Models

We are continually reviewing and revising our pastoral model, and that certainly holds true for religious education. It seems to me that a lot of education programs in the Catholic Church today are backwards. In other words, we try to catechize the children first, in hopes they will have a defining experience where they fall in love with Jesus Christ. Is it realistic to expect that from kids? I don't think it is. In the Acts of the Apostles, Paul gave communities an experience of the Risen Lord. Only *after* that did headquarters send out catechists and the "weekly envelopes." Doesn't this happen with the rest of us? We fall in love and then step back and try to understand what just happened. It *is* realistic, though, to expect that defining experience with Jesus from their parents, and that's what we focus on in our parish model. The truth is, the CCD model of religious education that's been around for years is broken. And it's now up to the pastoral imagination—to all of us—to figure out how to replace it.

After 9/11, there was only one airline, Southwest, that didn't cut back on its service, schedule, and employees. And it turned a profit the following year. What were they doing? They adopted a servant-leadership model. Sound familiar? They emphasized service. And their philosophy of servant-leadership was that middle-level managers needed to look at employees just beneath them—not solely at their supervisors—to make sure they were helping the most important person in the chain of command: the customer. In the church, we're appointed pastors, and we tend to ask ourselves, "What would the bishop want me to do?" More important, I believe, we need to be focused on the level below us, on *our* customers, to see how we can provide the best service to them.

No matter what model you adapt—whether it's servant-leadership or cultic, progressive, or liberal, whatever—nothing is as important as caring for people. People will forgive you for anything as long as you care for them and love them. Many of our colleagues have made a career out of doing nothing else. They've never run a program, never had an appointment; all they do is go to wakes and hospitals, and show up on Sundays. But many of them are loved. This brings me to the second major responsibility of being a pastor today, after being keeper of the vision: selecting your staff.

Optimizing Your Staff

I look for five basic characteristics in people I want on my staff. First and foremost, they have to like and have a caring attitude toward people.

The second thing I look for is work ethic. They have to work hard. If you're only working twenty hours a week, then you want to move to the next parish. A lot of people on our staff put in big hours. They work weekends, they work evenings. And if I have to do a lot of supervision, then we're both in trouble. I don't have the time to do that.

The third characteristic I look for is that they share my vision of the church. They have to be on the same page as I am, with my ecclesiology and where we're headed. They have to plug into my pastoral vision. I evaluate my staff each year, and as part of that process I typically do some coaching. I may say to a staff member, "How about lunch on Friday?" That gives us a chance to sit down and see how their plans fit in with those of the parish. Whether they're doing worship or youth ministry, or director of volunteers or outreach, it's important that we strategize with the end point in sight. I know what they did last year, but how are they going to fit into our church's plans for the year ahead?

The fourth thing I look for in my staff is a willingness to be part of a cohesive team. I have a particular aversion to people who want to look good at the expense of others. Internal rivalries like these can threaten that spirit of teamwork. If the dispute is small, I try not to get involved. But if it appears to be major, I'll step in. I don't like to take people aside and tell them what to do, however, because that relieves them of their responsibility. Now *I'm* the one responsible.

The fifth characteristic to search for is an area of expertise. That's not always possible in the people you inherit, of course, but it certainly *is* in the people you can hire. I look for each of them to be very good in one particular area. Often, they are the people who can see the big picture. They get it. Not everyone on the staff has to see the big picture. That's my job. But it really helps if at least *some* members of the team have that broad perspective—they have the expertise. I give these individuals a good deal of responsibility and control. I might say to them in a situation, "I'd be inclined to do it this way, but it's your call. I'll go with whatever you decide." And I do.

When it comes to hiring, I think you should hire from within the congregation, if you can. Let me give you an example. There was a woman in our parish who had a job with a large company, but who also helped to train my IT team when I lost the person who normally did that job. She was bright, articulate, spoke well before groups, and had a master's degree. The only thing she didn't have was parish experience or a background in catechetics. That was the easiest thing for me to "buy." I realized I'd be hard-pressed to find someone else with her talents and her ability to articulate her faith, so I made a decision. I hired her and sent her to school—and that decision has more than paid off. Sending people to school to get the training they need is one of the best investments we can make as pastors. Not every parish has the resources for something like this, but for those that do, it can have a profound effect not only on the individual employee but on the parish as well.

We need to be aware of our role as "talent scouts," you know, where we stand on the steps before and after Mass on Sundays, get to know the people, and size them up for possible roles in the church. Especially when it comes to volunteers, you can't just have your secretary call or send out e-mails. You have to ask people directly. And once people that you've scouted are on the team, it's your responsibility to nurture them and bring them along.

When I became pastor, I also served as youth minister since we didn't have money to hire someone. So I invited a couple of young adults in the parish to work with me, and we developed a team. The first year they watched me work with the kids. The second year we split the responsibilities, and the third year they forgot I was even in the room. By the fourth year these youth leaders had become so good at their jobs that I didn't have to attend their meetings anymore. I was able to devote that time to other pressing matters, like a church-building project that was underway.

Assessing Parish Needs

Let me turn now to the third and final overriding responsibility of the pastor, after keeper of the vision and selecting a top-notch staff: assessing the needs of the parish. Central to that job is meeting with parish leaders and the rest of your staff, and the entire parish, if you can. The first year I was a pastor I didn't do that. I met only with the parish council. Later on, I realized my mistake. So the next year I held a giant parish "senate" and invited everyone to attend. We held sessions on Friday night, Saturday morning, and Sunday afternoon to ensure the greatest attendance. And we held it in October which, along with November, is the best time to get people together. Because these months are outside the Advent/Christmas and Lent/Easter cycles, I think people hear us better. We also held information-gathering nights when people raised issues. Here, we used the affirmative inquiry method that comes out of Case Western University in the Midwest. That method says, "Start with the glass half full." We asked our people what they liked best about the parish, and then what they thought we could tweak, or do better. It's a chance to share dreams and designs, followed by implementation and evaluation.

One assessment of parish needs found that CCD just wasn't working, so we scrapped it and set up a "family faith formation" program. The result is these giant parish assemblies that we hold monthly. Children can't attend unless their parents are also there. There's lots of food, lots of time spent with mom and dad, and lots of presentations. In addition to these assemblies, we hold family learning sessions monthly and, on a less frequent basis, community sessions.

I think it's important as part of the assessment process that we as pastors stand up in front of the parish and enunciate what our "points of light" are—what our game plan is for the coming year. We should also provide a narrative on how the past year went. As part of that, we should prepare a financial statement, with the help of our finance and pastoral councils, and mail it to the homes of parishioners to make sure everyone gets a copy, and not just those who attend Mass on Sunday.

Annual study days with my staff are also an important part of assessing the needs of the parish. One of my most critical jobs is working effectively with my staff; we all have to be on the same page. So we explore questions such as "Where are we going?" and "Where's the pain in the parish?" ("Wherever there's pain" is a pretty good place for our ministry to begin.) I've found that this type of brainstorming session has an abundant payoff throughout the course of the year. I'm reminded of the saying, "If you fail to plan, you plan to fail."

Sometimes, effective planning means not creating new programs but letting go of ones that aren't working. For example, if the annual parish festival is just limping along, wasting your time and resources and not accomplishing much, then get out of it. I said above that our parish scrapped CCD because we found it wasn't working. We decided to go in a different direction, which can often be a lot more difficult and exhausting but, ultimately, more rewarding. Most important, be receptive to ideas from your staff, your congregation, even other parishes. If someone has a good idea, don't be afraid to adopt it. That's what effective pastoral leadership is about.

Endnotes

1. Bill Huebsch, *Dreams and Visions: Pastoral Planning for Lifelong Faith Formation* (Mystic, CT: Twenty-Third Publications, 2007), 65.

3

A Six-Month Game Plan

Jim Lundholm-Eades

How do you survive the first six months of your pastorate? Like any other job with wrenching responsibilities, having the right game plan in place will give you a vital springboard for long-range success, along with personal growth and satisfaction.

In the beginning, relationship building should be your number-one priority. There are experts who will insist you have to get finances, staffing, and sundry other things fixed. All of that is true. But above all, if you're going to fulfill your primary duties to sanctify, govern, and teach as pastor, you need a strong foundation for the long term. And that consists of the quality of your relationships. At the very outset, you'll get a free pass to do a few things, but until you've established strategic relationships within the parish, you're essentially on borrowed time. So, my first suggestion is to aggressively build those relationships.

The temptation when you first arrive is to get your feet wet in many different areas. But one of your immediate goals should be to sanctify. Indeed, if that's all you accomplish in the first part of your pastorate, no one is going to fault you. Parishioners and staff may pick on you for your staff choices or for your relationship with the new school principal, say, but if you're seen as a person of prayer, as someone who thoroughly prepares his liturgies and preaches well, someone who visits the sick and the homebound and is serious about outreach, then you'll get through the first six months of your pastorate in very fine shape.

Setting Personal Limits

Of the many spiritual virtues you've learned and been taught, exhaustion and burnout are not among them. We want you as pastors for the long haul. So you need to know, and set, personal limits. One thing about parish ministry is that the church will always ask for more. And if you don't set limits for yourself, no one is going to do it for you.

In the course of advising parishes over the years that were facing major problems, I've seen many pastors who were simply overwhelmed—emotionally, spiritually, and physically. That's why it's a good idea for you to check in regularly with someone who knows you well, a friend perhaps, or your spiritual director, or someone you went through the seminary with. Don't attempt this journey alone. And remember, too, there comes a time when you're allowed to say "No."

How Relationships Figure

In the course of building relationships, keep in mind that different types exist. A supervisory relationship, for example, is where you oversee a specific role, such as a staff member or volunteer from the parish. It's a hierarchical relationship; you're their supervisor. But that doesn't mean you have to give work directions to everyone. You probably have a business administrator and a school principal who get along fine on their own. In other words, you aren't responsible for everyone, nor should you try to supervise everything that goes on in the parish. Give others—including staff, lay leaders, and volunteers—the freedom to do their jobs. If you can't trust them to do that, then you probably have the wrong people in those jobs.

People believe that the employer-employee relationship can sometimes come into conflict with the pastoral relationship—resulting from the fact you serve as both their employer and pastor. Most of the time, they're not in conflict. But there may be times when it's advisable for you to suggest that an employee find pastoral care outside your embrace. Moreover, it's sometimes desirable if your employees not be your parishioners. That's not always possible, of course. In this case, you'll have no choice but to create a happy marriage between your roles as employer and pastor.

For example, I know of a case involving a pastor who let his music minister go because he was in the terminal stage of cancer and was unable to report to work. Learning of this development, the bishop approached the pastor and expressed dismay that he could dismiss this sick man and leave him bereft of medical insurance at a time when he needed it the most. The bishop in effect admonished the pastor for emphasizing the employer-employee relationship over the pastoral. Yet I know quite a few bishops who would take the opposite view. They would argue the pastor did what he had to do. As unpleasant as it was, he made a wise business and human resources decision.

As pastor, it helps to know the mind of your bishop and be able to act accordingly. The challenge is that decisions involving your dual role as employer and pastor are seldom black-and-white. They involve shades of gray. That's why my advice to you is to find someone who's been down this road before, like a fellow priest, and speak to him. His wisdom could be crucial in helping you find a practical solution.

Another type of relationship you'll encounter as pastor is consultative. In the public sector, this relationship is usually identified with organizations or bodies like school boards or city councils. But that's not the kind of model the Catholic Church has in mind. And the fundamental reason they're different is because the church is not a democratic body. When there's a consultative relationship between me as the layperson and you as the pastor, we're reliant upon each other, we're doing this together to discern the will of God. And the will of God is not necessarily spoken by majority rule.

Keep Your Relationships Transparent

There's another dimension to some of the relationships you'll form that you should be aware of. It's really shaped around two parallel structures. On one side is the traditional parish hierarchy where the pastor presides over the various advisory bodies and his staff. In most parishes, however, there's a much more informal structure built around the people you play golf with on Mondays, for instance, or parishioners whose houses you go to regularly for dinner. These individuals also wield influence within the parish, even though they aren't part of the formal structure. There's certainly nothing wrong with these informal relationships, but they can become a problem if they're kept out of sight and shielded from the traditional structure—if there's no transparency, in other words.

Let me give you an example. Let's say you're talking with your pastoral council about the need for a new parish center, and a parishioner you're friendly with is filling your ear with reasons why the center should not be built. My advice to you is this: get that conversation into the right forum. Suggest that your friend have coffee with the chair of the pastoral council and talk about it. To help you steer clear of internal politics and accusations, make sure there's transparency between the informal and the formal structures. Make sure the two sides are talking to one another.

Make Mission an Ongoing Dialogue

When it comes to shared dialogue, there's no greater imperative during your first six months than to promote a common understanding of the mission of the church among your various consultative groups. These include the pastoral council, finance council, and school advisory committee or school board, depending on what you call it. Make sure all these groups are in sync with the key variables that impact mission, including parish finances, the physical condition of your buildings, and staffing needs.

What I'm going to tell you next will surprise you. Don't do a mission statement—at least not immediately. What I'm suggesting is that when the focus of your consultative bodies is on producing a mission statement, you're engaged in a terminal conversation. Once you've written that statement, any dialogue on understanding the mission of the church is over. It's finished.

Here's what I suggest instead: capitalize on your role as teacher to initiate a broad discussion that breaks open the mission of the church universal, then moves to the mission of the diocese and the mission of the parish. If you *then* choose to do a parish mission statement, do it within that rich context so it becomes part of an ongoing dialogue—not a terminal discussion—about mission.

Building Trust

Another piece of advice to guide you through your early months is, make a conscious decision to operate from a position of trust. But don't confuse trust with naiveté. Trust your staff, your parish leadership, and your parishioners, but make sure your eyes are wide open and that behind your trusting smile is a little bit of savvy and a healthy dose of skepticism.

Also, beware of parishioners bearing agendas—or sharp teeth. These individuals don't belong on consultative bodies, particularly when they're driven by self-interest. Ignatius had it right. One of his prerequisites for the process of discernment is to have an open mind. That's critical for any consultative body in the parish.

Building trust also means being able to separate fact from opinion. When you're new, people will tell you endless facts about your parish. Most of them aren't really facts, but opinions. Take with a grain of salt statements such as "This is the way we've always done things here" or "No one would ever agree to a change like that." I'm not saying people intentionally lie or mislead. They just have different perspectives, and you must be mindful of that.

Earning Authority

From day one, you'll enjoy authority by virtue of your appointment by the bishop. It's an "authority of position." And if there's ever conflict in the parish, you can defuse it with the statement, "Because I'm the pastor."

Like everything in life, though, authority changes. After you've been with the parish for a while, people will assign you authority because you've demonstrated that you know what you're doing, that you're competent. Interestingly, one of the things I've observed in beginning pastors is the fear they'll fail because they *don't* know what they're doing. And they don't want others—especially their fellow priests—to be aware of this fear. Try to rise above those insecurities and realize that the people around you really want you to succeed. And they're only too willing to assign you authority because of the competencies you've shown, because they believe you know what you're doing.

People will also give you authority because of the relationships you've built—which underscores what I said above about relationships being your number-one priority. You can play the "Because I'm the pastor" card once or twice, but what will carry you from the time you enter the parish until the time you leave are your competencies and the quality of your relationships. Indeed, your sanctifying and pastoral care roles are crucial. If you've helped people as pastor and you've been kind and loving in your relationships, then parishioners don't really care if you're not a financial expert. They'll give you authority because you've earned it.

Governance vs. Management

It will help you as new pastors to be able to separate governance from management. You were not trained to manage. You were not ordained to manage. But pastoral governance uniquely positions you as teacher and as keeper and articulator of the mission of the church at all levels.

I like to think of this dynamic in terms of a "governance box" with four sides and a bottom. One of the sides is Catholic teaching, where you say to people, "Stay within the teachings of the Catholic Church." A second side is financial sustainability, where your overriding message is, "We have to live within our means." A third side is the mission of the church universal, which requires you to stay focused on mission and purpose. And if you can't relate your activities to the mission of the church universal, then you should probably stop doing them. The fourth side is the personal preferences of you, the pastor.

Let me explain this. You're the boss and have the right to do things, like the liturgy, a certain way. That's part of your governance authority. In the corporate world, it would be the equivalent of a new CEO coming in and exercising his preference for an orange carpet and dark blue walls in his office. By the same token, you can exercise as pastor your personal preferences as they relate to Catholic teaching, to financial sustainability of the parish, and to the mission of the church universal.

Residing between the four sides of the governance box is the temporal space known as "management." It consists of programs, procedures, and tasks. You should try to stay outside of this box. That's not always possible—physically, mentally, or emotionally. But as much as you can, stay focused on governance—on financial sustainability, Catholic teaching, mission, and personal preferences—the things you were ordained to do. Put another way, learn to maximize governance and delegate management.

The Levels of Delegating

So, what exactly are you delegating? There are different levels. You delegate tasks to some people, mainly because that's their comfort level; they can't handle much more than that. To others, you delegate functions, and to still others, you delegate or authorize relationships; for example, you delegate your director of religious education to relate to all the volunteer catechists.

As pastor, you also delegate authority. Your business administrator, for example, is authorized to sign checks in your name up to a certain amount. In addition, you delegate power and control to others, such as your youth minister to run all the youth programs in the parish.

One thing you can't delegate, however, is your role as pastor. You can't delegate sanctifying, preaching, and teaching. You can't delegate governance.

Limit Your Priorities

Research has shown that a highly functional parish with the right staff and the right leadership can handle four or five priorities at a time. When you're new to the parish, however, your focus should be on one or two—and if you're really good, perhaps three. For example, your focus this year might be on faith formation and the quality of music at Mass, but not on youth ministry and fundraising for a new building.

So, limit your priorities, and here's a way to do it. When you enter the parish, keep a notebook handy on your desk, and at the end of each week, or even at the end of each day, list the top three, four, or five priorities you saw lived out in your parish over that period. And on the second half of the page, list what you think the priorities of the parish should have been. Is there any difference between your two lists? This is a tool that I've found a lot of pastors—both new and experienced—consider very helpful. It's a way of asking yourself, "Are we doing what's really important?"

This exercise has even greater value when you consider the fact that we in the church have a hard time saying "no" to anything. "Oh, that's a good idea. We should do that." Here's an example. In my diocese, Catholic Charities had eighty-seven programs ten years ago and was going broke. None of those programs was being done well, and the organization suffered from what I call "mission creep." Recognizing the problem, the director of Catholic Charities conducted a rigorous review of all eighty-seven programs and narrowed them to five. Today, each of those five programs is efficiently run, and the organization has plenty of money.

You can achieve the same results at the parish level. Pretend you're an outside observer peeking in at the activities of the parish over the past week, and ask yourself, "What priorities stood out?" Then view the same landscape through your eyes as pastor, and ask, "How did I spend my time this week? What priorities was I focused on? Were they the right ones? Should I change my focus?"

To Change or Not to Change

Here's a good tool for deciding whether or not to change something in the parish: think of a flat horizontal line, representing amplitude. Then think of how much that line might deviate from the median—like a wave—if it were set in motion. High amplitude. Low amplitude.

When you see something in your parish you think needs changing, look at it as an amplitude line. How far off-center—how far from the median—is it? Is it a lot, or just a little? And that, in turn, will depend on how often it occurs—is it a one-time or frequent occurrence—and whether it impacts a lot of people or a relatively small number.

If it's low amplitude—meaning it's not happening often and is only affecting a small number of people—it probably doesn't belong among your top priorities for change. But if it's high amplitude—meaning it happens frequently and impacts a lot of people—then pay close attention. For example, you may find upon entering your parish that there are some liturgical practices that aren't your first preference. But measured as an amplitude line, they aren't that far off the median. So, my advice is leave them alone through your first six months, or your first year. Don't mess with them. You have more important things on your plate.

Remember, you don't have to have a response to every issue or an answer to every question. During your first six months, here are some really useful phrases: "I don't know." "I'll have to think about that." "What do you think?"

The volume of materials and information you get as a new pastor is just mind-boggling. You can't assimilate all of it. How do you separate the urgent from the important? Here's one simple way, which I refer to as the "pocket trick." If I'm walking through the corridor of the parish and someone stops with a suggestion, I'll write it down on a piece of paper I carry with me and put it in either my right or left pocket. The right pocket means I'm going to act on it, the left pocket means it's going to be filed away. Either way, the individual making the suggestion is pleased because I wrote it down. I'm listening to the person, but it doesn't mean I have to act on everything. It's okay to ignore some things in the interest of time.

Some of the best advice I ever got in my career was from a very successful school principal, whose job I took over. He told me, "There are very, very few issues that need to be resolved or questions that need to be answered today." And sure enough, I've seen time and again where even if the financial situation you inherit as pastor is troubled, you have time to turn it around. You really can't be blamed for financial woes for at least two to three years.

Separating Fact from Opinion

While the honeymoon will last for a while, what you should be doing immediately is making sure you're receiving sound financial information from multiple sources, including your finance council, parish staff, non-parishioner professionals, and the diocese. Be aware that everybody will volunteer opinions, but very few people will give you cold facts. And sorting out fact from opinion when it comes to parish finances is one of the greatest challenges you'll face in your new role.

You can meet the challenge head-on by asking the right questions of the right people. Go to financially savvy people in the diocese and on your parish staff and ask them probing questions like, "How are we looking for the next one to two years?" "Do we have good financial controls, procedures, and policies in place?" "How well do they work?" "Can they be improved?"

An even more important question to ask after arriving at the parish is this: can we meet our obligations—including payroll, utilities, and funding our ministries—over the next six months? At the same time, you need to understand your long-term obligations. Pertinent questions to ask here include, "What are our revenue and expense trends for the next two to three years?" and "What long-term debt obligations do we have?"

If you've got a handle on those, then you've got a handle on most things temporal. And even if finance isn't your strong suit and you can't read a balance sheet, don't worry about it. Somebody on your parish finance council can. It's more important that you be able to see the big picture.

Conclusion

To recap, your first six months as pastor will be an exhilarating—and exhausting—period of your life. Rest assured you'll make it, but it helps to have a thoughtful game plan. And that short-term plan should focus on building strategic relationships; sanctifying; governance over management; identifying priorities, both current and future; setting reasonable boundaries and limits for yourself; listening broadly but not reacting hastily to what people tell you; being trustful, but with a dash of skepticism; separating the important from the urgent; and relying significantly on the authority of relationships, like the one with your bishop, for day-to-day-matters.

Getting Started:
The Parish Business Office

Maria Mendoza

It's not uncommon for a newly appointed pastor to walk into his parish and be overwhelmed with financial and administrative challenges. In some cases, parishes are running huge deficits, accounting systems and budget procedures are outdated, and there's very little, if any, financial oversight. In short, things are out of control.

Not the vision you had in mind when you accepted your pastorate. I'm sure you saw your ministry as tending to the spiritual needs of parishioners, not to the financial and maintenance troubles of the parish. But the reality is, once you become pastor, administrative and financial issues are impossible to ignore. As the temporal side of your house, they demand your attention as well as a level of understanding and strategic thinking if you're going to effectively deal with them.

Your First Steps

What should a pastor do the first time he sets foot in his parish? I've geared my remarks to help you answer this question and get through those tough early days as administrative chief. And nothing is more critical to a smooth transition than having open channels of communication to your parish staff and parishioners. One strategy that worked very well for our pastor when he was appointed was establishing chat sessions with members of the church. This gave our pastor the chance to get to know parishioners and for them to become comfortable with him. It also opened the doors to a useful exchange of ideas.

Because I had an accounting background, the pastor asked me if I could help out on a part-time basis. I agreed, and I remember that one of the most challenging tasks during the early chat sessions we held was explaining to parishioners about the financial straits our church found itself in. Nobody really knew because the numbers had never been reported to them. But because we were now being very communicative and honest and open in our discussions with the parish, the support we received from the congregation was wonderful.

When you enter your parish and try to make improvements, members will invariably come to you and say, "This is the way we've always done things. Why change?" And that's a difficult and even scary position for you as newcomer to find yourself in. My suggestion to you is this: listen carefully to them and acknowledge what they have to say. They may be right. Maybe you shouldn't make changes. But more important, don't be afraid to change established procedures if you're convinced that you're right.

For example, one of the changes we made in our parish—and it's relatively simple—was restructuring our office hours so that our small staff had more time to get work done without parishioners walking in the door. As part of that change, we also closed our office from noon to 12:30 so that our staff had time for lunch. And while some parishioners complained initially about the new office hours, it worked out well in the end for everybody.

When you consider any type of administrative change, the question you should ask is, "What are the benefits of this change versus the cost?" If you can't afford to make a change, then you certainly shouldn't. But you should also weigh the time commitment. Don't waste your time and energy on small or frivolous changes. Try to target major areas of expenditure and, above all, put the mission of the parish and the needs of parishioners first. Remember, administration is not about winning a prize for having the best practices and procedures in place. It's about supporting the mission of the parish. That's what your overriding goal should be.

Human Resources Review

Two major areas I feel you should be focused on at the outset of your pastorate are human resources and financial accountability.

With respect to human resources, I believe my parish can offer an instructive model. What we did was sit down with each key member of our administrative and pastoral staffs and ask, "What do you think your job is here?" That gave us an opportunity to learn about each person's qualifications, work experience, and educational background. This information was critical because we had to determine if each individual was really qualified to be doing his or her specific job. In one case, for instance, our due diligence resulted in moving one financial person to another position within the parish, and then hiring someone better qualified to handle those same responsibilities.

After we interviewed all our staff members, we met with the head of each parish ministry. It was important for us to get a complete picture of the roles they played and the goals for their ministries. That information, in turn, gave us a good overview of what the parish was doing and what its current and future needs were. It also served to point out the value of volunteers to our parish, since money was tight and we had to be creative when it came to filling positions. For example, instead of having one paid, full-time receptionist, we now have a network of volunteers. It took us months to arrange this, but it works great. The volunteers are all retired women who know the parishioners by name and love to come in and help.

Another idea we launched was tuition relief for our parochial school students. We have a lot of parents who have lost jobs and need help with tuition for their children. So, what I designed and put in place for the parish was a program called Tuition-Assisted Grants that asks these families to commit to jobs for perhaps a day a week within the parish in return for tuition relief. It's been a challenge to coordinate, but the program has proved very successful and has been well received by parents.

As part of your human resources review, it's important that you determine what kind of leadership style you're most comfortable with. Are you going to be a pastor who has a hand in every decision within the parish, or are you going to be a pastor who delegates and assigns certain duties to others? In our parish, the pastor is kept apprised of everything and has the final word. But decisions are made independently by the staff within certain guidelines that take some of the burden off the pastor's shoulders. Examples include the approval of invoices, the booking of parish facilities, and the procurement of office supplies and services.

Because your staff is such a vital asset to you as pastor, it's essential that they be kept happy, especially since salaries are not usually high.

Many of the staff work in the parish because they love the Catholic Church and its mission, and we try to create an environment where they can feel good working together within the construct of their faith. For example, we say a prayer before we start office hours each morning, and we have a staff-only Mass once a month. There are other personal touches like birthday cakes and occasional lunches for staff members. That kind of attention is important because there will be plenty of times when you need people to stay beyond their regular hours or go the extra mile on a project.

Toward Greater Financial Accountability

Beyond human resources, what you do to ensure financial account-ability in your early days will help set the tone for your pastorate and win the support and respect of your staff and parishioners. That's why it's important that you sit down with your accountant or a finance council member after arriving to review all the numbers. Have them explain to you what they mean, and what they say about the financial strength of the parish.

I would also urge every new pastor to go through an external audit. It's not something to fear. The auditors will come in and review all your internal controls and accounting systems. This is an important tool for you because it will allow you to start with a clean slate. The auditors aren't going to say to you, "Okay, you were at fault because you failed to do this or that." They'll advise you as to what they found and tell you what to do to correct any problems. When our auditor conducted his review of our parish after the new pastor and I arrived, the findings filled an entire book. It took us over two years to act on all the suggestions. But the immediate value of that process was huge because it allowed us to define the types of administrative jobs and duties we needed to fill.

Another area you need to pay attention to on the road to greater fi-nancial accountability is bank accounts. For starters, determine how many bank accounts you have, whether they're all needed, and if they can be consolidated. When I joined my parish, we had about forty bank accounts because every time the parish had a fundraiser it opened a new account. So it's important that you take inventory of all your bank accounts and make sure that the signature card for each account is changed to include you as the main check signer. Moreover, determine who the second check signer is since the parish may have had volunteers and others over the years whose names were never deleted as second signers. Now is the time to conduct a thorough review and bring those lists up to date.

In the interests of financial transparency, you should also prepare and update on a quarterly basis a detailed parish budget that's been reviewed by you and the finance council. Determine what the role of each ministry has been in preparing the budget. Also, make sure you distribute the budget through your bulletin or website, or mail it home to parishioners. As a final step, couple your budget exercise with an evaluation and update of all your long- and short-term plans.

Pivotal Role of the Finance Council

No group can give you a better financial grounding in your early months than your parish finance council. Its members comprise your advisory board on all financial matters. That's why it's so important to have the right people with the right skills and backgrounds sitting on the council.

I'd like to make several suggestions on who should serve on this body. Certainly you need people with finance backgrounds, like accountants and bookkeepers. But if possible, I also suggest you have someone with an engineering or construction background who can offer advice on buildings, grounds, and maintenance issues. Another professional you want to have on your finance council is a lawyer. In the event legal issues arise—over contracts signed by the previous pastor, for example—a lawyer can make suggestions on how to proceed. I'm sure you know how expensive lawyers can be. So it's always good to have someone with legal skills on your council, though it's not always easy to find someone.

It's also desirable to have someone with a marketing background. The reason is, if you want to increase your tithing, for example, or do a capital campaign and fundraiser for a new building, a skilled marketing professional can spearhead and provide the expertise for that program.

With respect to the operations of the finance council, I suggest you divide the group into different subcommittees to make its work more productive. These subcommittees might be budget and finance, buildings and grounds, and stewardship. You'll find that by delegating tasks to these various groups, resolution on important issues will occur more quickly, and you won't waste as much time at parish council meetings.

Know the Balance Sheet

I can't stress enough, too, the importance of reviewing monthly financial reports or statements that detail your revenues and expenses, receipts and disbursements, cash flow, and other indicators of how the parish is doing financially. As pastor, it's desirable for you to have at least some familiarity with balance sheets because they can give you a snapshot of your financial strength at any given time.

That knowledge can be extremely helpful when it comes to communicating with your congregation. For example, if your balance sheet shows a large cash reserve, you'll be able to specify whether it's "restricted" or "unrestricted." Why does this matter? Because not all cash is "available." Some may be in the form of prepaid tuitions by families or donations earmarked for specific purposes. If a good deal of your cash reserve is restricted or unavailable, it strips you of a cushion in the event of a bad year when expenses exceed revenues, or when you need funds for an emergency repair. In such a case, you'll have to find a way to finance your deficit or expenditure. And in today's tight credit environment, that's probably going to be a costly proposition for your parish.

Your review of the balance sheet will also tell you if any investment assets, such as stocks and bonds, are held by the parish. If so, review the investment policy for each asset. If there is no policy, establish one right away.

Also take a close look at any parish debt. Along with your accountant, determine why the debt was incurred, as well as its interest rate and maturity. Any repayment plan should be consistent with the financial condition of your parish. If it's not, you need to get together with your lender and try to hammer out a more favorable plan.

Spotting Revenue Trends

Another financial barometer you should be attuned to is the statement of cash receipts and disbursements. From this document, you can ascertain the parish's major sources of revenues and expenses. Typically, major sources of revenues are the Sunday, Christmas, and Easter collections. Go back at least five years in your review of collections to determine trends. Are they headed upward or downward? Or have they become stagnant? These indicators could show the need for a new tithing campaign, for example. Your collections are a pivotal source of revenue, so it's very important that you be aware of the trend lines. Indeed, if your revenues are going down and you're not doing anything to try to reverse that situation, then you're headed toward a possible crash. In addition to collections, many parishes depend on the stipends they receive from baptisms, Masses, funerals, and weddings to prime the revenue stream.

On the expense side of the ledger, the largest items for most parishes are payroll and employee benefits. Other major expense categories are ones regulated by the diocese: property insurance, auto insurance, diocesan assessments, and diocesan newspaper subscriptions. The challenge with many of these expenses—particularly salaries and benefits—is that they're fixed. It's not like a corporation where you have some cost flexibility. The church needs its employees and its teachers. And some dioceses, like ours, have mandated salary increases, giving you less room to control costs. What's even more troublesome is if your collections are stagnant or on the decline. In these cases, you need to be huddling with your financial folks and weighing meaningful action.

One final thought on finances. Be honest and open in imparting information—even if it's gloomy—to parishioners. Don't spring surprises on church members at the last minute and expect them to be in a charitable mood.

Maintain Your Physical Plant

Let's move from the ledger sheet to buildings and grounds. To start with, it's important as a new pastor that you do a walk-through of your physical plant to determine the need for any immediate repairs. You should be accompanied by your maintenance supervisor or custodian, as well as a member of your finance council. Be vigilant on this walk-through, ask questions, and take notes.

When I started at our parish, preventive maintenance didn't exist. As a result, nobody changed filters in the air conditioners, serviced the furnace, or caulked the windows. It seemed like everything was in stages of decay or disrepair. Making matters worse was the fact we didn't have the revenues to bring conditions up to speed. Our only option at that point was a capital campaign—which we did, entirely on our own. With a goal of $500,000, we actually raised nearly $600,000 over three years and were able to undertake a significant upgrade of our physical plant.

After you've done the walk-through of your buildings and grounds, develop a long-term maintenance plan if you don't have one or update any plan that exists. Determine if you have maintenance contracts in force covering infrastructure items like air-conditioning, furnace, water heater, phone system, and computers. Also, change the contact person and password for the fire alarm and security systems in case of an emergency. As pastor, you should be notified at all times of any emergencies. And for security reasons, determine who has keys to the parish buildings.

By staying on top of maintenance now, you'll ensure it doesn't become a financial albatross for your parish later on.

Parish Demographics Are Key

My last suggestion is that you make an effort to know your parish demographics. Ask when the last time a parishioner census was done. If none was done in the past five to ten years, think about asking the parish council to conduct one. A census can provide vital information for planning your religious education and youth ministry programs, for example. It's important to know how many young children and teenagers you have, and what their numbers are likely to be in the future. You may find, for example, that you have seven hundred children in the parish, but only one hundred of them attend Catholic school. Numbers like those could trigger an enrollment campaign aimed at growing your school population. A census will also show tithing versus nontithing parishioners.

Also make sure you have an updated parishioner roster. At my parish, we were using the services of a company that was sending tithing envelopes to everyone on the list of parishioners we supplied them with. We decided to do a study to see how current that list was and discovered that many people hadn't tithed in years. So we updated our roster by sending out a survey and saved considerably on mailing expenses.

One way to ensure that both you and parishioners are apprised of what's going on within the parish is through a website. Does your parish have one? If so, how often is it updated? Are you maximizing its value by including as much information as possible about the parish? The website provides you as pastor with a perfect platform for communicating with your congregation, as well as with the outside community.

Finally, congratulations on your appointment. Ninety percent of what you need to succeed as a pastor you've already achieved . . . your faith, hope, compassion, and eagerness to bring God's love to all people. As for the remaining 10 percent, find a good staff and make sure you're fully in touch with the temporal side of your house.

Developing a Comprehensive Human Resources Program

David Boettner

The relationship that exists between the church as employer and its employees, and volunteers at the parish level, is at once simple and complex. Many of our employees who help extend the healing touch of Christ are also members of the flock in need of the pastoral ministry of the church. Because we often pray together, celebrate First Communions and funerals together, and occasionally dine together, we all feel like we're part of a close-knit family or community, sometimes even referring to ourselves as a "parish family." As a result, the traditional lines between employer and employee often get blurred, and we tend to improvise and make things up as we go along, not unlike an old-fashioned mom-and-pop store. The problem here is that we can no longer afford to operate this way. The world we live in today demands that the church be transparent, accountable, compliant. Unfortunately, when it comes to the laws, rules, and best practices that govern employment, many times we are *not*.

The church sees the dignity of the human person as the fundamental and perennial heart of Christian teaching on human work, and so we need to look closely at how our theology should shape and inform the way we approach our roles as employers. To that end, I'd like to draw on the document *Co-Workers in the Vineyard of the Lord*, in which the United States Conference of Catholic Bishops states, "Best organizational practices are consistent with Gospel values."[1] In that spirit, I'm going to present for your consideration a comprehensive human resources system that comes straight out of *Co-Workers in the Vineyard of the Lord*—complete with some useful tools and instructional examples. In the process, I'll also touch on the concept of the church as employer and our own roles as supervisors of employees. Indeed, it's a role we need to take seriously and understand well if we're going to handle it in a responsible and effective way, a way that doesn't keep us awake at night.

Creating a Special Work Environment

Speaking for the Lord, Ezekiel once proclaimed, "The lost I will seek out, the strayed I will bring back, the injured I will bind up, the sick I will heal (but the sleek and the strong I will destroy), shepherding them rightly" (34:16, NAB). Those compassionate words form the basis for pastors' training in my own diocese of Knoxville, Tennessee. First and foremost, we are called on to participate in the ministry of our bishop in order to shepherd the people of God. When you become a pastor, you are also called to pastor your team of employees. They are not just a resource to be used, but people entrusted to you to help extend the healing ministry of Jesus. If you shepherd your staff well, they will in turn shepherd others well.

I recently hired a youth minister who had worked as a nanny. This young woman took care of two children whose mother had died and whose father really needed someone in the house on a regular basis to focus on the needs of his grieving children. He took very good care of her, even paying her for the weeks when he took his children by himself to see family out of town. He would say to her, "I want to make sure you are not worrying about your financial needs so that you can worry about my children."

In a sense, we need to see our employees in the same way. We need to meet their basic material and spiritual needs so they can focus on the ministry of the parish—so they can effectively reach out to the people who have been entrusted to our care. This begs the question: How do we turn our parishes into places where our employees love the work they do?

That's not an impossible goal. In fact, it *should* be our goal. We want our employees to come to work loving the work they do, feeling that it's meaningful and that they're contributing something worthwhile. But if we are to help them derive satisfaction from their jobs and enable the church to draw on their talents, ingenuity, and creativity, then we have to focus on the *whole person*. We don't really want our employees to perform their work robotically. As a church, we believe that the basis of the value of work is the individual and that work should enable them to become "more a human being," and not be degraded by it.

In his book, *The Eighth Habit*, Stephen Covey talks about developing the *whole person*, including mind, body, heart, and spirit.[2] This whole person paradigm is important. People need to learn. They need to live. They need to be loved. And they need to leave a legacy. The church, as it turns out, is uniquely equipped to address each of these needs. By engaging people in their work, we stimulate their minds through growth and learning and help their creativity rise to the surface. By providing them with a fair wage, we help ensure their basic material needs are met and that they're able to focus on their jobs and their families. To love and be loved is the most essential human need that gives meaning and purpose to our lives. By treating them kindly and making them feel loved, we touch their hearts. And by using their gifts to serve human needs in principled ways, we help ensure they're making a difference through their work and that they're leaving a legacy.

As pastors, we have a special role in developing the whole person. It's a role we are uniquely equipped to carry out. I believe that each of us became a priest for at least three reasons: community, identity, and mission. We wanted to belong to the community of the church and to be people of communion reaching out to others. We wanted to be identified with something bigger than ourselves, and we wanted to do something meaningful with our lives. We wanted to have a mission in life.

I believe our employees aspire to the same things. We need to help them see that they're not just reporting to an office each day, that they're part of a community of people with a unique identity. They need to know that they have an important role to play in extending the ministry of the church, to reach out to those who are in need and those who are seeking a closer relationship with Christ. We want them to be able to proudly say, "I work for Sacred Heart Cathedral" or "I work for Blessed John XXIII parish." By focusing on the whole person we help our employees "share by (their) work in the activity of the Creator."[3] If they can embrace this sense of community, identity, and mission then we truly are doing something meaningful as pastors.

Developing a Comprehensive HR Program

Co-Workers in the Vineyard of the Lord articulates six distinct components of a comprehensive human resources program—components that I'll briefly outline here and then discuss in more detail below.

1. *Recruitment and selection.* We need to find qualified, motivated people who have a desire to collaborate with us in ministering to the people of God.

2. *Orientation and support.* We can't just hire people, give them a desk, and then walk away. When we bring people into the parish, we have to orient them and help them become an integral part of the parish culture and environment.

3. *Evaluation and feedback.* We have a moral obligation to give people reliable feedback on their job performance and help them to see areas of growth and strength so that they can be effective in their jobs. Critical to this process are thoughtful and thorough job descriptions.

4. *Compensation.* We're accustomed to think that because people work for the church, they should be underpaid. If we look at our Protestant brothers and sisters, that is not true. They actually pay very well—at or above market value. If we put our minds to it, there's no reason why we can't do the same. A wonderful resource for pastors is the National Association of Church Personnel Administrators. I would encourage you to join this organization so you can access their website which contains job descriptions and salary and wage scales for specific jobs that are broken down by regions of the country. It also compares that data with other Catholic churches in your area and with the nonprofit sector.

5. *Transition and termination.* This is always a difficult area because it involves conflict, and we've essentially been conditioned to believe that conflict is bad. Actually, it can be an opportunity for growth. As pastors, we consistently have to deal with conflict. If we try to run away, it only gets worse. That's why we have to have the courage to face difficult situations that may involve conflict and to do so in a loving way that conforms to the Gospel. Even if the situation involves an employee termination, you can—and should—handle it with love and grace.

6. *Grievance procedures*. A realistic grievance procedure requires that the church commit itself to listening to all parties in a conflict through well-known and clearly communicated processes. A grievance procedure ensures the basic right of all the faithful to due process.

The components of this human resources initiative can also be adapted to volunteers who serve our parishes. Instead of recruitment and selection, what we're really doing is *helping them hear and respond to the call* to service, much like we did as priests. Orientation and support could more accurately be called *formation* in the case of volunteers. You can't just stick volunteers in a job; you need to form them and help them to be successful. Volunteers also need to be evaluated, and they need feedback in order to become more aware of their strengths and weaknesses. Instead of compensation, there's *appreciation*; hosting volunteer dinners or finding other ways to recognize volunteers' hard work can have a tremendous payback and should not really be an option.

As for transition and termination, it is possible, of course, to fire a volunteer. It is a difficult task, yes, but something that may have to be done if the individual is sowing conflict and division in your parish. What is more helpful is to have regular terms of service for volunteers so that there is a constant cycle of succession and celebration of gifts given.

And finally, instead of a grievance procedure, there's accountability. As pastors, we need to be held accountable for our actions and the actions of others. If there are just two words that I think all of us as priests, and especially as pastors, need to incorporate into our ministries, they are *transparency* and *accountability*. If we don't get those right, then we will continue to see ourselves taken to task and, even worse, we'll do a poor job serving Christ and his church.

Resources to Back Your Talent Search

As pastor, you'll encounter no more important—or challenging—task than hiring qualified, talented people to serve your parish. That's why you need to have a full complement of resources behind you. The HR specialist in your diocese is a good example. I'm aware that many times we as priests tend to look upon the chancery or the diocesan office as "them." But they really do want to help us. We give them a good deal of money in our assessments, after all, and should take maximum advantage of the services and expertise they offer. Employee recruiting and selection is no exception, which is why I urge you to make an appointment to see your HR specialist.

You should also take a close look at your parish's job descriptions for staff members. If you're like most parishes, job descriptions will be skeletal or nonexistent, in which case you'll have to create them. Be aware that a job description is not just a document, it's a vital communication tool and therefore needs to be reviewed and updated regularly based on your annual performance review process. You need to critically assess if each description is an accurate representation of the job, or if it needs to be modified to fit changes that have occurred. Once again, the National Association of Church Personnel Administrators can be helpful. This group has compiled a comprehensive manual of job descriptions, along with appropriate salary ranges.

Another vital tool in your hiring process should be a search committee, which you'll have to appoint if one is not in place. Our parishes are full of talented laypeople who could serve as members. One of my own parishioners, for example, is human resources director for a large hospital corporation, and I call on his expertise frequently. Find people in your own parish who have managed companies or HR departments, or who have experience in hiring or counseling within the private, public, or nonprofit sectors. Try to make sure, too, that your search committee has people with experience in parish ministry. Once this search committee is in place, have members review the job descriptions with you, making sure they're consistent with the actual parameters of the job. Also discuss with the committee salary requirements, keeping in mind that the benefits package could add 30 percent to the total job compensation, a fact most people don't realize.

The purpose of the search committee is to assist you, so be sure to use its services. Don't attempt to do everything by yourself. Delegate a member to post job openings on websites, parish bulletins, and diocesan papers. Name someone else to collect all incoming resumes—ideally, someone with experience in the field so they can initially screen and weed out applicants whose qualifications do not match the job requirements. This can be particularly valuable given the number of resumes you're likely to attract in a high-unemployment economy. Another bit of advice based on my experience with parish hiring is this: respond to every resume, no matter how qualified or unqualified the applicant seems. Always thank them, and if they're not a viable candidate let them know as soon as possible so they don't waste their time and yours.

A word on posting open positions: if you are not familiar with Catholicjobs.com, you should be. It's a great website on which to advertise jobs, especially ministry positions. There are many other popular websites, such as monster.com, that can serve as valuable job-posting resources for your parish, especially if you're looking to draw younger candidates. Many dioceses also have job-listing services on their websites. Your goal should be to get the widest exposure you can so you can encounter the best candidates available.

Uncovering the Best Candidates

What kind of candidates does your parish want to attract? This is a question you and your search committee should carefully consider. Clearly, you don't want to hire anybody just to fill the slot. You want the best and the most qualified candidates because the people of God deserve nothing less. So set your sights high and ask, what are the Gospel values this individual needs to demonstrate to make the job meaningful to everyone in your parish? And if you don't find the right candidate at first, be willing to start the whole process over again. There are many other qualified candidates out there if you have the patience and perseverance to look.

Once you start interviewing, remember to check references carefully. Failure to do so can be a big mistake. It's important to know a person's work history and see what kinds of references they list. If they volunteer only personal references, not business, that could be a signal of possible problems in the past with employers.

Let's talk for a moment about the interview process itself. Again, your search committee can be instrumental once you've determined which candidates merit follow-up. Develop a list of interview questions and have members conduct phone interviews with those candidates, rating them on a predetermined scale. That will enable you to narrow the field even more before you spend time and money bringing people in for personal interviews.

Prior to face-to-face interviews, I would encourage you to take advantage of a computerized assessment tool. These are pre-hire tools that help you to find the best-matched candidate for a particular job.

We use Profile XT in our parish which helps us to interview and select people who have the highest probability of being successful in a role. It also provides practical recommendations for coaching employees after they are hired. These tools draw upon the job descriptions and benchmarks you've established to map out specific questions that will help you determine if a candidate is right for the position. If you're looking for a youth minister, for example, you want to be able to assess the candidate's energy level to see if they have the stamina and drive to handle the rigors of that job.

Make sure, too, that you give interviewees the chance to ask questions. It's not a bad idea to ask them, "What do you want to know about us?" Viable candidates are those who have done their homework. They've been to your website, studied your parish, know the job description (because you sent it to them in advance), and know what questions to ask.

If the position involves handling money, you should also consider conducting a financial background check. If a candidate has a significant amount of consumer debt, for example, it might show patterns of decision making that you should be aware of, even if they don't necessarily disqualify that individual. Check the laws of your state before conducting a financial background review. Your diocesan HR people can help you here.

Speaking of money, if you find you're not attracting the pool of candidates you really wanted, you may have to take a second look at your compensation scale. Churches and nonprofit organizations are often conditioned to think, "We really can't afford to hire this person." But consider that mind-set for a moment. If we can't afford to hire the right person, can we really afford to hire the wrong person? Is that going to make us stronger? I know how difficult budgets can be. But remember, when we hire quality candidates, when we have talented people and effective staffs working for us, our parishioners will attach great value to that and respond accordingly. This may require taking your case directly to them. If you tell parishioners, for example, "In order for us to have a full-time youth minister on our staff we need to raise our weekly gift giving by one thousand dollars," you may be very surprised at the response you get.

To sum up what I've just covered, I believe a third of your focus should be on developing a solid job description, a third on assessing all resumes you receive, and a third on conducting an exhaustive interview with the candidate. You might discover that based on a resume alone, a candidate does not measure up 100 percent to the job. But when the personal interview and profile are considered, they may show growth potential that deserves special consideration by you and your search committee. You should always keep your options open.

Smoothing the Transition

Let's talk for a moment about getting new employees up to speed. Because the first year on a job is so critical, you need to be actively involved in integrating new employees into your staff so they can become effective and productive members. If you can devote the time and energy to a meaningful transition, you'll be helping to ensure a long-term, loyal employee who is a wonderful addition to your parish.

My own transition to one assignment didn't go that smoothly. I showed up on a Sunday night after the previous pastor had moved out. There was no furniture in the rectory. I didn't have keys to the office, so I had to wait until it opened the next morning. And when I got to my office, there was no computer and no chair. That is the opposite of what you want to aim for!

One suggestion to make the new-hire process smoother is to find someone in your parish who can make a "welcome to the team" gift basket and present it to the new staff member. Engage other staff members in putting balloons or a card on the new hire's desk to welcome him or her and show that the new person is a valued member of your team. You might also hold a social of some sort to reinforce the greeting. Make sure that you or someone you designate schedules time at the start of employment to present the new member with a policy handbook from your parish or diocese. Make sure to meet, at least quarterly, with your new hire to review progress and listen to the person's experiences during the transition. A good on-boarding process takes at least one year.

And finally, don't forget to say "thank you"—not just to newcomers but to all members of your staff. It's easy as a pastor to get so caught up on day-to-day issues that you forget the impact those two magic words—thank you—can have. People thrive on recognition and affirmation. Last year we took our employees to a nice restaurant for an employee appreciation lunch, and I received more thank-you notes for that event than for any of the raises we handed out that year.

Reviewing Employee Performance

Every pastor should ask the question "How do we help people reach their full potential and gain satisfaction from a job well done?" During an employee's first year and at least twice a year after that, you need to give attention to evaluating the person's performance. Essential to that process is an accurate job description, which I mentioned above, so that you know the criteria against which you're evaluating the employee.

My advice is to keep the performance review simple. Your goal should be to establish a dialogue that not only reveals areas where you've noticed the employee is doing good work but those where the person needs improvement. An effective performance evaluation must cover both—successes as well as personal growth opportunities.

If you've had issues in the past with a particular employee, you should work hard to resolve them and move on so they don't become chronic problems. If those conflicts persist, you may need to move in a difference direction with the employee. In cases like these, it's wise to prepare what I call a performance improvement memo (see Appendix A, p. 171). It's just a simple form that explains in writing what the problem or issue is, how the employee needs to improve, and what the consequences will be if that improvement is not seen. Be sure to document everything. More and more employees are suing the church over alleged employment abuses, and no one is exempt. The more fully you document your interactions with your staff, the stronger your case will be if it becomes a legal matter.

Compensation

Just treatment of workers includes fair compensation for the jobs they perform. The standard for fairness is greater in the church than in the regular workplace because we believe each employee should make a living wage with health-care, sick leave, vacation time, and provision for retirement. This is based upon the social justice teachings of the church. While it is a challenging standard, it is in keeping with Gospel values and best practices. If employees' material needs are not met, they will never be able to fully engage in the work that's been entrusted to them. With respect to salary, we need to be concerned that our employees at the very least make enough to meet their basic needs of food, shelter, and clothing. But we also need to pay attention to what the market around us pays for a comparable position, as well as what other churches pay. This will position us to attract and keep the best employees.

You should keep in mind, too, that benefits can add as much as 30 percent more to the value of a position. Benefits are not an option but a necessity for fulfilling the Gospel and for maintaining a talented workforce. I suggest preparing a Total Compensation Worksheet (see Appendix B, p. 172) so prospective employees can get a better understanding of all the costs that go into a compensation package. This worksheet could also be used as a tool to help current employees see that the resources spent on them by the parish is far greater than what's reflected in their paychecks.

Letting Employees Go

Among the most difficult tasks you'll face as pastor is letting someone go. Heed the advice of a company in my own hometown: "Hire slowly, fire quickly." To be sure, there's nothing worse than dragging out a termination that should have been done months or years earlier. At the same time, a termination should never come as a surprise or shock to the employee, unless it's over a major issue such as theft or gross insubordination. In most cases, you have a moral obligation to keep the employee aware of what's happening at every step of the way, to give them opportunities to change and improve their performance.

If firing an employee becomes necessary, don't approach it with anger or bitterness but with compassion and love. Help them realize the relationship is not working and that a change is necessary. Also, offer to help them with their transition through salary consideration or benefit assistance so that it's not a traumatic event for them. Be as generous with severance as you can afford to be. And finally, always have a witness with you at the time of termination. Never do it alone. Contact your HR department to see if they can help. If they're not able to, find another staff member or a reliable parishioner, possibly a member of your pastoral council or finance board, who's had experience in this sensitive area. Make the termination meeting short and factual. It is best to have a written script of what you plan to say and give that document to the employee after the meeting so there is no discrepancy about what was said at the meeting. Finally, be sure that both you and the witness write down everything about the termination meeting immediately afterwards so that you have it on file.

Grievance Procedures

Having a written and well-known policy on how employees are to handle conflicts in the workplace is critical to fostering a just environment. In our diocese, the chancellor and I are usually the recipients of grievance issues. We attempt to facilitate open discussions of the issues that arise. Many parish employees feel they are in an unequal power relationship with their pastors and thus don't feel comfortable addressing concerns to them. Part of the responsibility of the diocese is to enable Christian communities to follow the Gospel in how they work together to resolve disputes. The best model we have comes from the Gospel of Matthew 18:15-20. The first responsibility of any party in a grievance is to go directly to the person they have a grievance with and speak with them—not to win the argument but to gain a better understanding of each other's position. The procedure for redress in canon law follows the Gospel by sending the injured party to the person who has caused them harm before they can move to a higher level. In situations of alleged harassment or abuse, there must be a place for people to direct their concerns so that action can be taken to respect the rights of all employees.

I would encourage you to think through possible scenarios with your staff in order to design a policy that can be used in your parish for conflict resolution. It's important to resolve conflicts at the lowest level possible to prevent them from dividing your parish. Many conflicts are a result of poor communication. For its part, the Archdiocese of Saint Paul and Minneapolis set up an office of conciliation that could well serve as a model for other dioceses and parishes (see Appendix C, p. 174, for an overview).

As a fellow pastor, I can assure you that the more you know, and the more tools you have at your disposal, the more comfortable you'll be in your new role of responsibility. No one is expecting you to turn into a human resources dynamo, but by developing and executing the kind of comprehensive HR program I've outlined, you can become a more effective manager and leader of people in service to your parishioners and to Christ.

Endnotes

1. United States Conference of Catholic Bishops, *Co-Workers in the Vineyard of the Lord: A Resource for Guiding the Development of Lay Ecclesial Ministry* (Washington, DC: USCCB Publishing, 2005), 61.

2. Stephen R. Covey, *The 8th Habit: From Effectiveness to Greatness* (New York: Simon & Schuster, 2004).

3. John Paul II, On Human Work (*Laborem Exercens*), §25.

6

Risk Management

John McGovern

As surely as the seasons change, we know we're going to encounter risks in life. That's why managing them in an effective and proactive way is so crucial to your role as parish leaders. No one can eliminate risks, but one can minimize them and keep them from spinning out of control.

Unfortunately, risk management forces us to step outside our comfort zone and think like lawyers, accountants, businessmen, insurance agents, contractors, and more. It forces us to wear a variety of hats and look at things differently than we otherwise would.

In discussing risk management, it's helpful to start with a number of guiding principles. First, good fences make for good neighbors. In other words, good rules, policies, and structures make for good employees and volunteers within the parish. When we develop rules that are concise, fair, and clearly understood, we get much better results out of our people. They become, in effect, good neighbors.

Second, an ounce of prevention is worth a pound of cure. We can do lots of little things now to prevent big problems later on. Put another way, we can manage risks before they turn into crises. Proactive steps such as financial controls, monitoring, audits, and inspections are far more preferable than lawsuits, bankruptcies, and devastating newspaper headlines.

Third, controlling risk will not make you friends. No one likes rules and regulations. Your employees and volunteers will look upon them as restrictive and unnecessary. But you still need to have them in place, and they need to be enforced.

Fourth, risk management is a form of stewardship. Because we're put in charge of great assets, we must relentlessly care for them. If we don't, we run the risk of squandering them.

Fifth, we need to be aware of "third parties." These could be outside people or creditors who can initiate lawsuits or visit other problems upon us if we're not vigilant. For example, if someone gets hurt on church property and doesn't have adequate insurance to cover their medical bills, the hospital may come after us. So, we need to think not only about the people directly involved but about others who add secondary layers of risk.

With that as background, I'd like to turn to three broad areas of risk management that are particularly important to all of you as pastors and leaders of your parishes. They are legal, financial, and general risks.

Keeping Your Buildings Safe

Physical plant is the source of countless legal headaches. That's why I strongly recommend an annual inspection of your facilities. Physical plant inspections should include sidewalks, stairs, masonry, roofing, windows, and the like. There are many building inspectors who do consulting on the side who can help you with this. Or you may be able to take advantage of parishioners with special skill sets in the construction field.

It's smart to include funds for annual inspections of your physical plant in your operating budget. Somebody needs to routinely get up on the roof to ensure it's not leaking; somebody needs to inspect the windows to make sure they're working properly; and somebody needs to check the walkways and steps for loose bricks that could cause people to fall and break a limb.

Also be aware of your responsibilities with respect to any vendors you hire. Because of the potential for lawsuits, you need to insist that these vendors not compromise on safety—that they strictly follow OSHA regulations and not leave dangerous electrical cords, for example, strewn across areas where people are working. You should have a current certificate of insurance on file before you hire any vendor. Remember, these certificates are only valid for one year, so requesting certificates annually from vendors is extremely important. It's not a bad idea, either, to have these certificates mailed directly to you from the contractor's insurance company to ensure they're not forged or doctored.

Being smart legally also means documenting all occurrences on church property. Someone might slip and fall, get up and say they're okay, and you think that's the end of the matter. That's a dangerous assumption. The reason is, that individual has up to two years after the incident to initiate a lawsuit, and if they decide to do so and the incident wasn't fully documented, you could find yourself on very shaky legal ground. So, when any type of incident occurs on church property, it's best to document, document, document. That means getting a name and phone number, taking a picture of the site where the incident occurred, and getting the names and phone numbers of any witnesses. Just because someone walks away from a fall doesn't mean you should let your guard down. You need to be proactive at all times.

I'd also advise contacting your insurance company, even if there doesn't appear to be a serious injury. Someone trying to scam the system could suffer a back injury working in their garden, say, and try to pin the blame on a totally unrelated incident, like a fall at your church. Your insurance carrier might want to reach out and contact the party involved to make sure documentation is in place to head off any future wrongful claims.

Targeting Lawsuits by Employees

Let's turn to the employment arena, another fertile field for lawsuits. Those suits could be triggered by alleged age discrimination, gender discrimination, ethnic discrimination, or sexual harassment. Typically, they don't have clear black-and-white lines and are very difficult to manage.

Termination procedures often factor into employment-related lawsuits. So, if you're going to terminate someone's employment, you need to have a well-defined process based on solid documentation. That process needs to clearly spell out why the individual is being terminated, along with source documents to prove it, whether they be complaints or evidence of excessive absenteeism, tardiness, poor performance, and so on. Those documents need to be part of the employee's updated file.

It's always advisable to draft an "exit" letter when you terminate someone. It should state all the relevant facts, including the reason for termination and what documentation is available to substantiate it. Finally, the terminated employee should be required to sign the letter, and both of you should have a copy. This way, if a suit alleging discrimination on your part is filed six months or a year down the road, you have an accurate record of what the issues were and why you took the steps you did.

It's not a bad idea, by the way, for your parish to have an employee manual that describes in straightforward language the terms of employment: policies, expectations, vacations, sick leave, and so on. What's more, every employee should sign a letter stating they're aware of, and have a copy of, the manual. Such a document can be pivotal in the event a lawsuit is brought against your parish.

Among the key areas your employee manual should cover are policies governing sexual harassment. Clearly, your parish should have in place a zero tolerance policy so that there's no question in anyone's mind what constitutes sexual harassment. It's particularly important that the pastor set the tone here, and if you see or are made aware of any behavior or practice that violates the sexual harassment policy, that you deal with it quickly and forcefully.

Mitigating Contractor Risks

Tax issues surrounding independent contractors is another high-risk area. When you hire someone and don't withhold taxes, you run the risk of improperly classifying them as an independent contractor, instead of as an employee. A true independent contractor is someone who maintains a business with a physical location, phone number, clients, insurance, and so forth; they may or may not be incorporated. If you have any doubts, take a look at the checklist the IRS has prepared to see if they qualify as a business or as an employee.

Be aware that if you hire someone as an independent contractor and the IRS says, "No, they don't meet the criteria," then the parish will be responsible for that worker's full tax burden, including income tax withholding and Social Security taxes at the federal level, and disability and unemployment at the state level. And those taxes are going to end up costing you an additional 30 percent of what you're actually paying that individual.

Worker's compensation is another major concern when hiring a contractor. As a general rule, independent contractors are not covered under the parish's worker's comp policy; only employees are covered. So, let's say you retain an accountant and he falls down the front steps of the church and is injured. The parish's worker's compensation policy is not engaged; the accountant must use his own insurance. That's why whenever you hire an outside business, you should ask to see their certificate of insurance to make sure they're covered. Be particularly wary of undocumented workers and businesses. While your heart may be in the right place in giving the cleaning lady a job where you pay her without taking out taxes, you could be taking a huge legal risk if she is not independently insured as her own business.

Let me describe for you the magnitude of that risk. The State of New Jersey has a rule known as treble damages for worker's compensation claims. If the cleaning lady you've retained falls down the stairs at your parish, for example, and winds up at the hospital with no insurance, that hospital could end up spending $50,000 out of its own pocket to treat her. The hospital will be reimbursed from a special state fund created for cases like that, but in order to replenish the fund, the state will bill you, her employer, $150,000—treble damages, or three times the amount of the claim.

To reiterate, everyone who works at the parish must either be on the payroll system as an employee or have their own business with insurance coverage.

Financial Risk: Cash Management

Let's flip the page and look at our second major area of risk management: financial.

One of the ripest areas for trouble is the handling of cash, especially the proceeds from the Sunday collection. Specifically, you should have multiple teams of counters, and the same team should not count every week. Rotate the teams so that it's easier for you to spot any irregularities from one week to the next. In addition, all parishes should be using sealed and tamperproof bags for depositing collection proceeds, instead of the traditional canvas bags with the big zippers. Banks are on notice that if a seal is broken, they should not accept that deposit.

I also recommend that at least two of those counters sign the actual deposit slip. And here's the reason: if you're making a five-thousand-dollar deposit and have a signed slip to prove it, then this acts as a deterrent to a bookkeeper or anyone else from filling out and bringing to the bank an alternative slip for four thousand dollars and pocketing the difference.

Tight cash management should be employed for not only Sunday collections but also for school cafeteria money, bingo receipts, carnival receipts, and any other church event or activity where money is involved. Carnivals, in particular, can involve the handling of tens of thousands of dollars. So again, it's important to use sealed bags, teams of counters, and signed deposit slips.

You might think of cash as toxic waste. It requires extreme precautions in terms of how it's collected, where it's stored, who has access to it, and how it's transported. You also need to train your personnel in proper handling techniques. And to that end, you should have comprehensive procedures in place. It gets back to what I said above: good fences help to keep everyone honest.

Simple Ways to Detect Fraud

Speaking of procedures, one of the smartest you can adopt as pastor is to personally open every bank statement that comes in. In fact, no bank statement should be opened by anybody other than you. The reason is that you want to be able to take a close look at the bank's record of checks written by the parish to payees or vendors. In one recent scam involving a church, the names of legitimate, recognizable vendors were entered into its computerized financial books, but the actual checks were made out to individuals who fraudulently cashed them and kept the money, which eventually turned into a fraud of over $800,000. The scam was set up so that anyone looking at only the electronic records would never be able to detect it. The best way for you to combat this type of fraud is to scrutinize the checks and names of payees on the church's bank statement.

This practice should be applied, by the way, to every bank account you maintain, whether it's for the CYO, religious ed, home school, or any other. Experience shows that those small accounts can often be breeding grounds for fraud. Here's an example: you might go through your bank statement and see a check from the home school account written out to Sears for two thousand dollars for a high definition TV. When you question the head of that program, she tells you, yes, she wrote the check out to Sears but then paid it back with a personal check so that no one was cheated. She just wanted to avoid paying the sales tax on the TV. Well, at the very least what she did was defraud the state as well as misuse church resources. Again, a little vigilance on your part can help uncover these types of schemes.

Another good financial safeguard is to compare actual to budgeted expenditures. In other words, compare what's actually spent by a department against what it was budgeted for at the beginning of the budget cycle. If you have a maintenance supplies budget of five thousand dollars, for example, and halfway through the year your janitor has already spent ten thousand dollars, it's time to ask some hard questions. I'm familiar with a case involving a maintenance man who was taking church supplies and selling them every weekend at a Pennsylvania flea market and pocketing the money. A budget comparison can be helpful in spotting this kind of abuse. What can really help you in this effort is commercially available software that makes the budgeted-to-actual-expenditure comparison quick and simple.

It's not a bad idea, either, to have an accountant on your parish finance council. And be sure to ask that professional to conduct some random audits. Just knowing that someone is looking over their shoulder should help to keep all staff members on their toes.

Being Proactive about Unpaid Tuition

The final area I want to mention under financial risk management is unpaid tuition within Catholic schools. This is becoming an increasingly serious problem as more and more parents are out of work, and their discretionary money continues to shrink. The result is that tuition gets paid late or not at all.

While as Catholics we're sympathetic to the plight of these families, we can't turn our backs on the financial implications it has for our schools. We must address the problem proactively by establishing a policy around tuition delinquency and letting parents know upfront that if they fall x-number of months behind on their payments, their children will no longer be able to attend school. Or you might specify that no child is allowed to graduate unless the tuition is paid in full. Your parish may have a "tuition angel" type program in place to help needy families. But it's important to make sure these policies and programs are known in advance by everyone. Once a family has fallen two or three months behind on tuition payments, it becomes a very difficult process to manage once the unpaid tuition becomes substantial.

Another sound piece of advice is this: if a delinquent family decides to make a lump-sum payment, require that it be in cash or a bank check. This way you prevent a situation whereby parents write a large tuition check, allowing their child to graduate, knowing full well that check is going to bounce. They've managed to abuse the system because we weren't more diligent.

Managing Contractors

Beyond legal and financial is an array of other risks you're likely to encounter as pastor. One of the biggest involves building renovation and construction projects. Because these projects can run into millions of dollars, I strongly suggest hiring what's known as a "master of the works." This is an individual with extensive construction experience whose job is to keep an eye on the general contractor and ensure that appropriate materials are being used and that no shortcuts or variations from original specs are occurring. Because the master of the works keeps the contractor on his toes and helps mitigate or prevent potential problems, he's well worth his fee. You might find a retired person or a parishioner with considerable construction knowledge and background who would be delighted to serve in this important risk management role for the church.

When it comes to mitigating risk, sometimes it's better to just tear down a building. The Catholic Church has lots of old structures, and sometimes they're so antiquated and/or asbestos-filled that there's no point in renovating them or even letting them stand. As the parish leader, you may need to make that determination as a way of cutting your risks.

Raffle games are another area that can get you in trouble if you're not alert. Make sure that any organization you team up with to run the contest is following all gaming laws and regulations, particularly as they relate to obtaining proper gambling licenses from the state and distributing raffle books across state lines. We had a case of a pastor running a super-raffle who apparently didn't know any better and mailed books all over the country, in clear violation of U.S. postal laws. Also, make sure that you and any cosponsor are following federal tax laws, which require sending 1099 and W-2G tax forms to any raffle winner of more than six hundred dollars, whether it's in the form of cash or a prize like a TV.

Keeping Computers and Information Safe

Let's talk a little bit about computer risks, particularly in the area of backups. I can personally cite the case of a business manager who was diligent in backing up all her files, only to become the victim of an overnight robbery at the rectory that not only resulted in the loss of her desktop computer but also a box of backups that she kept nearby. The message is clear: all the backups in the world are worthless unless you secure them off-site. Robbery isn't the only risk: if a fire occurs in the rectory and the sprinkler system goes off, your backups could be destroyed. Still another example: we had a bookkeeper who dutifully backed up everything but inadvertently left her portable flash backup drive in the computer at the close of work one day. When she returned the next morning, she discovered that a lightning strike had fried the computer and her backups, including the flash drive. So watch how your staff handles the backup of important information.

Three other computer areas you need to be aware of are firewalls, spam, and spyware. With respect to the first, you need to be sure that your tech people have built a firewall that's capable of preventing intrusions into your network and the loss of propriety and personal information. It's important, too, that firewalls be tested on a regular basis by experienced companies to reduce the chance of a hacker breaking into your system.

Spam is also a serious problem because of what may be attached to it—software that captures and sends out propriety data residing on your network. In a more mundane way, as most of us know, spam can clog your machines and make them work much slower.

By the same token, spyware can pose a severe threat. Once this software secretly penetrates your hard drive, it can collect bits of personal information and monitor your computing function. The way to combat this intrusion is through installing anti-spyware and anti-spam software. Remember that it, too, needs to be regularly tested and updated to remain effective.

Let's conclude our discussion on risk management by turning to disaster plans, which any parish with a school needs to have in place. Lockdown procedures are an important part of that plan. Lockdowns are emergency protocols designed to protect people from a dangerous event originating outside your facility, like an intruder trying to break in, or from the inside, like a chemical spill in the science lab.

Lockdown procedures need to be practiced through periodic drills so that your principal and teachers have a firm grasp of when to shut the school down and when to keep students inside or send them outside the building. Remember to submit your disaster plans to the township and the chief of police.

The drills and precautionary measures you take may seem at times like an inconvenience or annoyance. But like the other forms of risk management we've touched on, they're a vital safeguard that protects you, the parish, and your people.

Risk management really *is* a form of good stewardship and one that you and your staff need to take quite seriously.

Best Practices in Parish Internal Financial Controls

Charles E. Zech

Let's start by agreeing to a basic premise: the church is not a business. We do, however, have a stewardship responsibility to use our resources as effectively as we possibly can to carry out God's work on earth. Sometimes carrying out that stewardship responsibility requires us to use sound business management practices and tools. But we can never forget that we are not a business. Operating like a business is not our goal. Pastors are not accountants. You have to have a little bit of understanding, though, so you can lead in the right direction those folks who *are* accountants. So, what I'll address are things designed to protect and benefit you.

A couple years ago I decided to survey Catholic diocesan chief financial officers. My real goal was to learn about diocesan finance councils, which appear in canon law but are never really studied. Several CFOs said to me, "Why don't you throw in a question about embezzlement or fraud?" At first I said no, but I finally relented and put one in the survey. And what I found was startling: some 85 percent of U.S. Catholic dioceses had experienced fraud or embezzlement over the last five years. Well, the press picked up on that and ran it. It was all over the newspapers across the country, which was not necessarily good, and a number of bishops voiced their displeasure. But it happened to be the truth. And it begged the question: why do we see embezzlement in so many churches today?

My answer was this: *because we tend to be too trusting.* People I know on the business side of the church say they're appalled at the lack of internal financial controls in most parishes—which arises from being too trusting. No one would think that a worker in a parish would steal money. No one would think that a volunteer would steal money. No one would think that a priest would steal money. And so we fail to put in place all of these internal financial controls that are common in the business world today. Let me be clear about this: It's to your advantage to make sure they *are* in place because if questions ever arise about someone's integrity—possibly your own—you'll have the proper internal financial controls and records to respond to them. If you don't, there's always going to be some level of suspicion—which is the last thing you want as a pastor.

After the survey was released, I was frequently asked by the press, how do Catholics stack up with Protestant churches when it comes to embezzlement? And I replied that it was probably about the same, since Protestant churches face the same basic problem we do: they're too trusting. The truth is, Catholic fraud tends to be blown up more by the media because we're larger, and there's usually more money involved—often millions of dollars. But secondly, we as a church do a really good job of ferreting out fraud, which is reflected in higher numbers. That doesn't necessarily mean we're any worse than our Protestant friends.

Parish Finances: A Great Concern

As part of the survey, I asked diocesan CFOs how good they were at collecting data in a cost-effective manner. Eighty-six percent said they were "very good" or "excellent." We then asked them to rank the greatest financial risk faced by their diocese, and 36 percent said potential litigation was number one. That wasn't all that surprising, given the fact the survey was conducted in 2005 at the height of the clergy abuse scandal when many dioceses were getting sued. What *was* surprising, though, was the fact that almost as many CFOs—34 percent—reported that their greatest worry was finances and controls at the parish level. They considered that to be a time bomb waiting to go off.

You would think one way to address that concern would be to just audit the parishes: conduct an internal audit where someone from the diocese audits your books, as opposed to an external audit where someone from the outside, such as a Big Four accounting firm, comes in. And what we found was amazing. Only 3 percent of dioceses audited their parishes annually, and 21 percent of the dioceses seldom or never audited their parishes. The most common reason to conduct an audit was a change in bookkeeper or pastor.

If I were ever appointed pastor, I would tell my diocese in no uncertain terms, "Before I get there, I'd like you to audit the books." Make sure you're starting with a clean slate because you don't want to be accused of something that happened three, four, or five years ago due to the actions of a parish staff member or volunteer who is no longer around.

Preventing Fraud

We also asked on our survey about submitting data regularly to the chancery and found that most dioceses do a pretty good job. When it came to fraud and embezzlement, however, only 39 percent of the dioceses had a formal written fraud policy requiring a possible theft to be reported to the diocese. When you officially take over as pastor, you should find out what the fraud reporting policy is in your diocese, or if it even has one. If you have a fraud in your parish, you should report it immediately to the diocese and let them worry about it. Hopefully they'll have a plan of action in place.

Keep in mind that when people commit fraud against a church, it's usually for small amounts at the beginning. They find a way to steal two hundred dollars so that no one will find out. The next month they steal five hundred dollars. When no one finds out, they up the ante to one thousand dollars, and it really starts building. So I urge you, if you suspect fraud of any type or amount, take immediate steps to stop it.

Who discovers fraud? Well, pastors are the most likely people to uncover it. But our survey also showed that the parish bookkeeper, internal auditor, parish finance council, and external auditor were also instrumental in detecting fraud. That's why it's so important to have an internal audit on a regularly scheduled basis, as well as an external audit. I wouldn't recommend an external audit every year, because it's expensive, but every few years is advisable.

To their credit, the U.S. Catholic bishops have taken this area quite seriously. Back in 1995, they approved a document titled *Diocesan Internal Controls: A Framework*.[1] I would advise you to become familiar with it, not because you work for a diocese but because much of its content can be applied at the parish level. So, find out where the document has information that would be helpful to you, become familiar with it, and, more important, make sure your parish business manager or your parish finance council becomes familiar with it too. If I were a pastor, I would want to make sure that my parish was doing everything this internal controls document spells out. It's a very good guide put together by both bishops and finance professionals, and I think you'll find it very beneficial.

Beyond that document, the bishops passed a resolution in November 2007 that directly addressed the issue of diocesan audits. At the expense of blowing my own horn, the CFO survey I did and its findings on embezzlement were in large part responsible for the resolution, which was passed by the USCCB's Ad Hoc Committee on Diocesan Audits. It called for, first of all, annual internal audits of each parish, meaning the diocese audits the books. An annual financial statement signed by the pastor and all parish finance council members should also be submitted to the diocese.

In addition to audits, I can't emphasize enough the importance of having a good parish finance council. So many parishes I know have a rubber stamp council. They do whatever the pastor wants. Don't let that happen to you. Make sure your parish finance council takes its job seriously and that its members are qualified for it, because if you follow the resolution of the bishops on diocesan audits, parish finance council members must affirm in writing, along with you, that the financial report and budget you're submitting to the diocese accurately reflect the financial condition of the parish, and that you've received no credible reports of fraud or misappropriation of funds.

So, you can clearly see the importance of the parish finance council to you and to the church. Make sure you have the best council you can possibly put together. And that typically means having a variety of folks on the council who look at things from different perspectives.

Managing Parish Performance

I was so intrigued by the responses we got to our survey of diocesan chief financial officers that I decided to extend it to the parishes. I got a grant and was able to work with an organization at Georgetown University known as CARA (Center for Applied Research in the Apostolate). We did a nationwide sampling of parishes and got back 632 responses. We actually surveyed both parish finance councils and parish pastoral councils, but I'll discuss our findings from finance councils only.

We wanted to see how well the parishes were living up to the USCCB recommendation that they have an annual budget and a comprehensive budget process. What we found was that 90 percent of parishes in our sample have an annual operating budget and that the parish finance council was involved at some level in all but two percent of parishes.

The responsibility of both the finance council and the pastor ultimately stretches beyond the budget. You must also conduct regular financial statement reviews. When our survey asked parishes how often they review periodic cash receipts and disbursements, almost three-quarters said at least on a quarterly basis, though 15 percent never do it. As for year-to-date cash receipts and disbursements, again 75 percent do it on at least a quarterly basis, though 10 percent never do it. On the question of how frequently they review unpaid bills at the end of the period, nearly half do it at least quarterly, though 39 percent said never. Another important finding was in the area of how frequently parishes compare actual to budgeted numbers. Our survey found that seven percent never compare what's actually happening to what they've budgeted. You and your finance council should have that information in front of you all the time. It should be part of your visual dashboard.

The next survey question focused on comparing current to prior year performance—a helpful piece of information. And again, 7 percent of parishes never do it. Nor do 11 percent ever review the amount of debt outstanding. Certainly, every parish finance council should be on top of those numbers.

The Case for Transparency

This brings us to the issue of transparency. You need to protect yourself, to be open and unambiguous about the state of the parish finances, and one way to accomplish that is to communicate the minutes of your parish finance council meetings to parishioners. It doesn't have to be a blow-by-blow description, but at least it should give folks an idea of what's going on. For example, don't spring on them from the pulpit two weeks before the close of your fiscal year that you're running a fifty-thousand-dollar deficit, and you'd appreciate it if they could put a bit more in their envelopes. Let them know early on that things aren't looking too good, so that you can do a better job of planning. Give them an idea of where the parish stands financially so that they can help you. Share with them the parish finance council minutes.

In our survey, we found out that 40 percent of parishes make those minutes available on request; 16 percent publish them in the parish bulletin; 3 percent post them on the parish website; and 1 percent mail them to homes. Significantly, 48 percent do not share them at all with parishioners. So much for transparency.

How about communicating with parishioners on the budget? Our survey showed that 76 percent of parish finance councils in preparing the budget asked the different ministries for a budget request. I was thinking 76 percent sounds pretty good, but then I realized: How can you possibly make up a budget without getting the ministries involved? How can you not go to them and say, "Okay, choir, or okay, education, what are you going to need for the coming year?"

No less critical in terms of transparency is the need for a preliminary budget to be presented to the parish pastoral council. You have these two important yet very different consultative bodies in your parish. The parish finance council is full of professionals who specialize in that area. The parish pastoral council is full of folks who have a good feel for the parish but who may not be professionals in the same sense as their finance counterparts. As Monsignor Casale will say, the pastoral council's primary role is planning. And to do that job effectively, they have to know what's happening financially in the parish. As they plan and see where the plan is going, and as they decide what can and can't be done the following year, they need information on the budget. And they need it sooner rather than later—which means keeping them apprised of what's happening with the budget at the preliminary stage. You shouldn't just hand your parish pastoral council a budget at the end of the process and say, "Okay, here's the budget for next year, you guys figure out what to do." It's not fair to them, and it's not fair to you. That's why it's rather disconcerting to know that our survey showed only 49 percent of parishes—not even half—present a preliminary budget to their pastoral council.

I urge you to keep the communication lines open between these two very important organizations. It's not a bad idea to have some overlapping membership, if it can be arranged. I know that some parishes make the finance council a subcommittee of the parish pastoral council. I think that's a bad idea. They should be equal. Indeed, the parish finance council is provided for in canon law.

Opening Up the Budget

There are other ways, of course, to communicate with parishioners on budget preparation. One way is to explain it in the parish bulletin, which 14 percent of parishes do, according to our survey. Another is to explain it at Mass, which 10 percent do. Frankly, I don't think that's a good use of Mass time. What I *do* think is a good use, though, is to hold open budget hearings where everybody in the parish is invited to attend. The pastor is there. The parish finance council is there. The business manager, if you have one, is there. And each organization steps up and gives its request—its budget—for the next year. That's really healthy because it disciplines these organizations to be more careful preparing their budgets. If you're a pastor, you know that every organization and ministry needs 25 percent more than they have this year. So what typically happens is, they'll throw that number out there and make you worry about where the cuts should be made. But if there's an open budget hearing, the organizations have to explain and justify *why* they need this increased funding. And it's good for parishioners to be there to hear and see what goes on behind the scenes. They're much more apt to walk away saying, "You know what, this process is really good. It's open, it's transparent, and it reinforces my faith in my parish leadership."

How many parishes today hold open budget hearings? A mere 9 percent, according to our survey numbers.

Let me warn you that whenever you open up a preliminary budget to the congregation, you're also opening a potential can of worms. That's because there are some parishioners who think that they should be the pastor, and they will come in and make their own recommendations on the preliminary budget. And if those recommendations are not adopted, they'll get upset; they'll be offended. Well, you just have to learn to deal with that. On balance, though, the benefits far outweigh the drawbacks of opening up the budget process to your parishioners.

How about communicating the final budget to your congregation? Almost everybody does that, as evidenced by the 99 percent of parishes in our sample share. They do it through the parish bulletin, 38 percent, and through oral reports at Mass, 33 percent. You heard me say before I don't like using Mass time to review the preliminary budget, but my opinion is different when it comes to the final budget. A few minutes spent talking about what's happening with the budget, the assumptions behind it, and so forth, is not a bad use of Mass time.

Though only 8 percent of parishes do it, posting the final budget on the parish website makes eminent sense. It's a great place to put things like that because it's available to every parishioner. As you start your pastorate, keep the website uppermost in mind for a wide range of communications chores, including the budget.

Following Diocesan Procedures

Transparency and accountability, as we just discussed, are major areas for change that emerged from the bishop's committee on diocesan audits in 2007. Other areas that can be directly applied to your situation as pastors are policy and procedures manuals designed to ensure that similar transactions are handled in similar ways. Many dioceses have done a great job of this: their websites are populated with their procedures for everyone to see. But how many parishes do this is problematic.

With respect to policies and procedures, our sample showed that about two-thirds of parishes use materials provided by their diocese. But one-sixth did not adhere to a diocesan policies manual, and a similar number failed to follow any accounting procedures manual. I think it's very important that your parish finance council use a diocesan manual for a couple of reasons. First, you have folks on your council who come from business, and they're not necessarily accustomed to doing things the way a nonprofit would, especially a faith-based nonprofit. And second, you need to follow a diocesan manual for consistency. It's tough on the diocese when parishes use different manuals and different approaches. It's important that there be some commonality, and I think all parishes using the same manual put out by the diocese is one way to achieve that.

I was recently in Des Moines talking about this very topic. The bishop there was trying to implement a common parish software program, and he found himself surrounded by angry priests who didn't want any part of it. I kept thinking to myself: it's to their benefit to learn this new software and to protect themselves by making sure everything is done according to diocesan standards.

Limit Bank Accounts and Check Signers

It's also to your benefit to strictly limit the number of bank accounts your parish has. This way, there's greater control and fewer opportunities for errors or wrongdoing. The poster child for this is the Diocese of San Diego. In 2007, it was involved in a lawsuit over the clergy abuse scandal, and the ensuing court case revealed that the average parish in San Diego had eight checking accounts, which meant that some had many more than eight. The truth is, you can't possibly control things in your parish when you have that many checking accounts floating around and that many people able to spend parish money. So it's really important that you limit the number of checking accounts. You could have a main checking account for the parish and different line items for each organization, like education and the choir. And when checks are written, it's your bookkeeper's job to know where the money came from and to be able to fully account for that expenditure on your books.

Here's another sage piece of advice: you should have a very limited number of folks authorized to sign checks, and checks of large amounts should require the signature of two responsible individuals, the pastor being one of them. You don't want to have eight people with the authority to sign checks because, obviously, you lose control.

Our survey showed that the average number of authorized check signers in the parish was only 1.4, and in two-thirds of parishes only one person was authorized to sign checks, no matter how large the amount. So, for example, the business manager or bookkeeper could sign a check for any amount he or she wanted. Let me be clear, that's really dangerous. It is how embezzlement starts.

Why Checks and Balances Matter

It's equally dangerous to have the same person depositing the money, signing the checks, and reconciling the books. Put another way, bank statements should be reconciled by someone other than the check signers in your parish. Our survey showed that 80 percent of parishes assigned the reconciliation task to one person, and in 5 percent of parishes that same individual had sole responsibility for writing the checks and reconciling bank statements. That's a bad practice and should be avoided.

We also found that in about one-sixth of parishes, the same person was solely responsible for depositing the Sunday collection and for reconciling bank statements. How tempting that must be—to pull some twenties out of the collection! In a third of parishes, one person deposited noncollection revenues—script, or revenues from fundraisers, for example—and reconciled the checkbook. That, too, is a bad idea. And finally, 40 percent of parishes gave one person sole authority to approve both routine disbursements and reconcile bank statements.

How about the Sunday collection count? As you undoubtedly know, that's another headache. In about 5 percent of parishes, according to our survey, only one individual counts the collection. About 40 percent employ a regular crew of counters, with an average of five members. Nearly half of those, however, fail to include any parish staff members among the counters. Both of those approaches are fraught with danger; the temptation for fraud or pilferage is just too great. Nearly half of parishes utilize a system of rotating counting teams, with an average of four members per team. Every week you have a different team, and if you see a spike or a dip in collections from one week to the next, it should raise a red flag for you.

It may be tough to implement a program of rotating counting teams, if you don't have one. That's because it requires telling people who may have been doing this chore for years that it's no longer good practice, that you're going to change things. They may feel insulted, and even say, "What, Father, suddenly you don't trust us? You think we're thieves?" The correct response is, "No. I'm doing this to protect you because if there's ever a problem and you folks are the only collection counters, you'll get blamed."

There's also the issue of supporting documentation. The message here is clear: if you're going to write a check, make sure there's documentation to back it up. Ninety-one percent of parishes in our survey required documentation to support each check they signed.

Finally, let me say a word about electronic funds transfer. It's a really good idea to encourage people—repeatedly—to use this medium for their parish contributions. Studies show the more they use electronic funds transfer, the more they give.

In fact, people who switch from nonelectronic transfers to electronic typically increase their annual contributions by 30 percent because of the commitment they've taken on. You can see why I'm such a big fan of electronic funds transfer. Don't forget, too, it's safer for everyone.

Your Stewardship Role

In closing, I'd like to stress the importance of drawing on the work the USCCB has already done. I've described for you some of the recommendations spelled out in its excellent handbook, *Diocesan Financial Issues*.[2] They include:

- rotating offertory collection counting,
- establishing fraud policies,
- annual internal audits supplemented by external audits at least every three years,
- public disclosure of the names and professions of every member of the parish finance council at minimum, quarterly meetings of the finance council to monitor parish and school financial reports,
- annual, and preferably more frequent, submission of financial data by all parishes and high schools,
- open, transparent, and accountable parish budget processes,
- encouraging parishioners to use electronic funds transfer for contributions, and
- anonymous channels for church workers and parishioners to report suspected irregularities or fraud

I'd like to leave you with this thought: the church is not a business, but it does have stewardship responsibility to use its resources efficiently. As local leaders of the Catholic Church, it falls to each of you to employ the best possible business management tools and practices to fulfill that stewardship goal. You'll be protecting yourselves, your workers, and your congregation while ensuring that your ministry is known for its accomplishments rather than for any financial improprieties.

Endnotes

1. USCCB, *Diocesan Internal Controls: A Framework* (Washington, DC: USCCB, 1995).
2. USCCB, *Diocesan Financial Issues* (Washington, DC: USCCB, 2002). It was revised in 2009.

Fundraising as
Christian Stewardship

Kerry A. Robinson

I was born to a family with a long and proud history of philanthropic support of the Catholic Church. My great-grandparents, John and Helena Raskob, made the decision nearly sixty-five years ago to set up a private philanthropic organization and designated the money to be used exclusively to support Catholic Church apostolates and ministries around the world. They also wanted their children and descendants to be stewards of the foundation's resources, and at last count there were nearly one hundred of us—including cousins, aunts, and uncles—actively engaged in service to the church as volunteers with the Raskob Foundation. All of us take this invitation and work very seriously and consider it a great privilege.

At the earliest age I can remember, I was introduced to this curious word "stewardship" and to assorted heroes and heroines—your brother priests and sisters in religious life and, on occasion, lay pioneers who were devoting their lives, just like each of you, in service to advancing the mission of the church. Just as importantly, I got to see as a young girl the Catholic Church from local, diocesan, national, and international levels and absolutely fell in love with it. I was struck by how all of you have given yourselves in service to a greater good, brought consolation to others, alleviated suffering, and advanced social justice. And whether you were doing ministry under very wrenching social conditions around the globe, or here in the United States, you possessed common traits which, from my perspective, were extremely compelling. One of those was a groundedness, a sense of purpose, and a deep faith. You also had a palpable sense of joy. And I remember thinking, I'll never be that holy, but if I could spend my life helping to advance *your* ministry, then my life too might be imbued with such purpose.

With that as background, it's an incredible privilege for me to speak to you about anything to do with the church, especially the importance of raising money.

Reared as I was in formal Catholic philanthropy, my role was essentially to advise on how best to give money away. I never, ever wanted to be responsible for raising it. I had all the biases which I think are still quite prevalent in the church when it comes to the task of raising money. That started to change about twelve years ago when I received a call from the Catholic chaplain at Yale University. Fr. Bob Beloin had just left parish life after being appointed by his bishop as chaplain at Yale. Among his first tasks were raising money and countering the fiscal distress, tending to crumbling and inadequate facilities, and increasing student participation, particularly at the Sunday liturgy. He called me and invited me to be the director of a five-million-dollar capital campaign, which I vehemently resisted. After all, I had no experience, knew I'd be terrible at it, and didn't even like the idea of fundraising, not to mention the fact I was seven months pregnant with my second child. Before I could decline the invitation, however, he asked me to pray about it for five days and call him back at the end of that period with my decision.

To my astonishment, after the allotted five days I called him back and said, "Yes, I will do it. But fundamentally, I don't see it as an opportunity to raise money so much as an invitation to advance and elevate Catholic campus ministry across the country by holding up a model of what a vibrant, intellectual, and spiritual center can look like at a secular university." There was a long silence on the phone, and Fr. Bob said, "I wish I had thought of that when I first called you."

Obstacles to Fundraising

Like many of you, I was forced to learn fundraising on the job, and the first thing I did at Yale was identify the key obstacles that prevented church leaders—people with passion, conviction, and vision—from being successful at raising money. I thought and prayed long and hard about this and examined my own inner self. The first obstacle I observed was that we have a theological ambivalence about wealth. Is it holy? Is it sinful? Is it only holy or sinful under certain circumstances? Until we focus on and resolve questions like these, I don't believe we can approach the activity of raising money without some level of cognitive dissonance.

The second obstacle I observed—and had a hard time believing—was the negative language associated with raising money. "Hit her up for money." "Put the squeeze on him." "Nail it." "Seal the deal." It seemed to me the expressions I was routinely hearing in connection with my new profession were really the language of violation, which is totally contrary to what it means to be a person of faith.

The third obstacle can be described this way. The Yale chaplain knew he had to raise money, saw it as a major focus of his apostolate, but had never been trained for this discipline at the seminary. Indeed, there was a radical disconnect between what was being taught at the seminary and the reality of coping with the day-to-day concerns and responsibilities in the temporal arena, particular anything related to money. So, a huge learning curve existed, and one of the things I discovered about many of the priests and women religious I've since worked with is that they look upon asking people for money as tantamount to a personal favor, rather than seeing it as an opportunity and a possibility to advance an important ministry.

The fourth obstacle to fundraising is one I've heard from priests many times: "I discerned a vocation to the priesthood to bring solace to others, to bring Christ to others, not to make them uncomfortable with subjects like their personal finances."

The fifth obstacle is fear or rejection. What if they say no? There is often the fear that if a prospective donor says no to my grant request, it's really a rejection of who I am and how effective I am as a priest.

The sixth obstacle revolves around the conviction that your real ministry is about something other than temporal affairs, particularly fiscal and fundraising, even when those are integral to church life.

To sum up, the activity of fundraising, even when seen as an essential component and chief responsibility of a pastor, is regarded as a distraction from his real ministry or, at worst, a contradiction of it. This is no small challenge, I'm sure you'll agree, when your mission includes raising money and ensuring the full financial health of your parish.

Fundraising as Ministry

How do we overcome these obstacles? What I propose is a radical shift in the way we think about raising money. The activity of fundraising is not a distraction or a contradiction to ministry but should be seen as an effective and profound ministry in itself. Let me give you an example of why I believe this is true.

I mentioned that our fundraising campaign at Yale was five million dollars. As we showed signs of success, the trustees raised the goal to ten million dollars. It often felt like a labor of Sisyphus, where we never quite reached the end. And yet we treated every prospective donor equally. We were so eager for *anyone* to show an interest in our vision—the vision of vibrant Catholic intellectual and spiritual ministry—that it didn't matter if they were capable of a small or large financial gift, or none at all. We believed that if our intentions were sound, some good would come of all of our encounters with alumni to discuss our vision of Catholic life at Yale. In the end, our most generous donors turned out to be the most unassuming, modest, and humble individuals.

The most important thing is that we treated development as a ministry and participated in animated discussions of a vision grounded in faith and benefiting others—one that was full of joy and passion and had the potential to outlive all of us. That conversation is an example of the great intimacy that takes place among the Catholic chaplain, the development director, and the donor prospect. We were touching the very core of what is meaningful in a person's life, and this new perspective on fundraising, as I like to call it, is not a contradiction to ministry. It embodies the important notion that donors are not objects from which we try to extract as much money as quickly as possible, but subjects who, like all of us here, are looking for something meaningful to do with their lives, something that blesses the lives of others and is well-conceived, well-articulated, and has merit and great possibility. Indeed, seeing donors as subjects rather than objects allows priests to approach the activity of development the same way they approach the rest of their ministry, which is with confidence, focus, attentiveness, humility, and joy. That important insight fundamentally changed the way we conducted our campaign at Yale.

Trusting in God's Providence

What also changed our focus was the realization that many of the key maxims to effective fundraising mirrored the tenets of spiritual maturation. Among them were hope, confidence, and a profound trust in providence. I'd like to illustrate the latter with the following story.

One of my tasks during the school semester was to go with Fr. Bob to meet with Yale alumni at their homes or offices. This often required us to travel to their cities, and on one such trip we drove two-and-a-half hours from New Haven to Boston to meet with this very nice prospective donor for about thirty minutes. He told us, "I applaud your vision, I like what you've accomplished, and I'll make a donation." We thanked him for his time and pledge, but on the long ride back to New Haven we spoke about whether the modest gift he made was worth the dedication of nearly a full day. I remember saying to Fr. Bob that the size of the gift was all a matter of perspective, and had it been day one of the campaign we would be celebrating wildly our first gift. Second, I impressed upon him that we have to have confidence that we're doing everything possible and working very hard. And while we can't predict the specific outcomes each time, we have to have the confidence and trust that some good will come from this dedication to purpose and hard work. Upon reflection, Fr. Bob agreed.

Fast forward six months. We received a call from a Yale alumnus who said he had just been to a party with a friend who had met with Fr. Bob and me in Boston, and he spoke glowingly of our programmatic vision at Yale. He went on to say that he wanted to meet with us with an eye toward getting involved. We held that meeting soon afterward, and the upshot was that this man presented us with a bequest for approximately five million dollars. Looking back, it's clear that contact would never have occurred if we hadn't faithfully and purposefully advanced our ministry of development. That kind of fidelity and trust in God's providence—coupled with incredibly hard work and tenacity—will invariably lead to positive results. And never losing sight of that fact is, I believe, a key to both successful fundraising and spiritual enrichment.

Money Follows Mission

This new perspective to fundraising also calls for a sense of joy. I mentioned above that what I as a child saw in your brother priests and women religious was a palpable sense of joy, a purpose, and an incredible closeness to God. Without joy, I don't think anyone can be truly successful in raising funds. Who wants to give to somebody who doesn't have confidence in what they're presenting or doesn't have a joyfulness about the possibilities at hand?

It's not so surprising that our overriding maxim became "money follows mission." The starting point for me, even in those five days of prayer when I had no idea what I was getting myself into, was that this was never about money. It was not an invitation to raise money but an invitation to bring to fruition all the possibilities at hand. And to articulate well and compellingly what our mission was.

As I grew in my new role, it almost seemed to me that the buildings we built and the money we raised were a distraction from our real work. And that was to hold up to everyone who had a vested interest in the future of the church a compelling example of a Catholic intellectual and spiritual center of excellence. I never once believed that our purpose was to reach a seventy-five-million-dollar goal or to build a thirty-thousand-square-foot Catholic center. For me, it was always about insuring that the bright and talented Catholic young adults attending Yale were properly catechized so that when they became leaders across every industry and sector around the globe they would be informed by the rich tradition of our faith, guided by Catholic social teaching and sustained and inspired by their faith. This was the overriding reason to get up every day and report to work. It was another shining example of the guiding principle I mentioned above: money will always follow mission.

The Call to Stewardship

A sense of stewardship has almost nothing to do with money, yet it's at the heart of every fundraising program. Stewardship can be defined as the proper care of all that's been entrusted to us. But I think it goes much deeper. Stewardship is the proper recognition of and care for what is possible, for the potential at hand. As Christian stewards, what we do with the potential for good in our midst—whether we ignore it by saying, "I'm too busy, I've got other responsibilities," or we act courageously on it, even knowing we might fail—is the mark of a wonderful, spiritually alive Christian steward.

If you think about it, over the past thirty or forty years Catholics have risen to levels of affluence and influence in this country that are staggering. They number among the highest echelons of leadership in every sector in the United States and abroad. This raises the question, "Why as stewards would we *not* want to avail ourselves and the church of the expertise, managerial insights, and communication strengths, as well as the financial and investing acumen, of these individuals who care so deeply about the mission of the church?"

We should strive for excellence across the board, even in areas where we don't feel prepared or proficient, including the temporal affairs of the church. And as part of that, we should be identifying Catholics who want to give back to the church. You would not believe how grateful so many of these men and women—who include executive leaders that compose the membership of the National Leadership Roundtable on Church Management—are. They feel a debt of gratitude to the church and want to give back.

The bottom line is this: giving what you do best in service to the church you love is so much more meaningful than writing out a check of any amount. What happens is, you become even more engaged in the mission of the church and the money eventually follows. Best of all, it's the purest example of evangelization.

So, try not to have the starting point of your efforts be about the collection totals but about reenvisioning a vibrant, relevant, welcoming, and exciting parish community. The world is hungry for that. And don't be afraid of identifying people who can move you toward that goal, and enlisting their leadership. Because when this endeavor takes on a life of its own, the money will follow.

I also think there are plenty of people who contribute to apostolates run out of local parishes who don't necessarily belong to them. And therein lies another opportunity. If you say to people, "This is what we're doing, here's where we're meeting unmet needs and responding as a faith community to a broken world," then you're giving them a chance to invest and be part of something that is such a hopeful opportunity.

Breaking the Mold

What often happens is, we get stuck in a maintenance mind-set. You know, we've always done it this way, so let's keep the tradition going. But the result is that it becomes stale, and then we have to ask ourselves, "Is our mission still relevant?" Because life changes, circumstances change. I'm sure as pastors you see this—or will see it—in your parishes. So, the question always has to be, "What is our mission, and how can we advance it in the most compelling, faithful, inspiring way?" When you operate with that mind-set as a community, you invariably take risks, you introduce novel ways of doing things, and you launch new initiatives. And when you start new initiatives that are faithful to the mission, the money always follows.

Another example from Yale makes this a little more concrete. We were in serious debt. But the response of the predominantly lay board of trustees before Fr. Bob came on the scene was to send a general appeal letter once a year that wasn't even customized. Not surprisingly, they weren't getting any responses to this very negative, generically written letter, and what happened over the course of ten years was that donations really ebbed. To make matters worse, the board decided to delete a huge percentage of the mailing list to cut expenses.

When we initiated our campaign, the first thing we had to do was massive damage control, and that meant finding those people whose names had been deleted and reclaiming their data. That strategy began to pay off—literally. One of our first million-dollar gifts came from a gentleman whose name had been deleted. In fact, he had never given before to Saint Thomas More Catholic Chapel and Center at Yale. Once we got beyond damage control, we knew that to be successful we had to be worthy in the eyes of prospective donors of their generosity. It wasn't fair to ask anybody to contribute to a campaign we wouldn't contribute to ourselves. So the starting point for us was to make sure that our mission was relevant, that we could communicate it well, and that we were actively advancing our mission in a manner worthy of generosity.

To that end, we began to introduce some bold new programs, like the one we called "Life as a Scholar and a Believer." It worked this way: once a month after the 5:00 p.m. Sunday liturgy, we would invite a Catholic professor from various departments or disciplines at Yale to speak, not about their scholarship but about their personal life of faith. Students were mesmerized by this first-of-its-kind program. They knew their professors were intellectual heroes and heroines, but they had no idea of the degree to which their personal faith informed their scholarship and their personal sense of vocation. Another attractive feature was that the program cost us almost nothing to run. We didn't have to fly in speakers or put them up in hotels. They were already on campus.

And guess what happened? When alumni around the country heard about the speakers program, they loved it and started sending in donations to support the chapel's operating and programmatic expenses. So it again illustrates several key points I'm hoping you'll leave with today: money follows mission, and successful fundraising means doing things differently from how they've always been done. Be bold and imaginative when the circumstances demand it.

Putting the Pieces Together

In addition to imaginative programs, it's critical that as fundraisers you assemble really competent people, both volunteers and staff. I frankly have a bias against professional fundraising companies. They're often expensive, and sometimes they're successful, sometimes they're not. I think it's better—though admittedly harder—to find an individual you have confidence in who possesses four essential strengths. First is being able to speak and write well. Second is showing drive and initiative and not waiting for a set of tasks. Third is being enthusiastic, passionate, and totally committed to the mission of the parish and vision of the campaign. And fourth is having somebody who is committed to and articulate about Catholicism and genuine in their love of the church.

Once you have the talent and programs in place and start thinking of fundraising as evangelization and engagement rather than as a distraction from your pastoral duties, then you'll be well on your way to a successful development program. As I've tried to emphasize, fundraising *is* ministry, and seeing prospective donors as subjects rather than objects allows us to approach our task with confidence, humility, and joy.

As Henri Nouwen stated in his book, *A Spirituality of Fundraising*, "From beginning to end, fundraising as ministry is grounded in prayer, and undertaken in gratitude."[1]

Endnotes

1. See Henri Nouwen, *A Spirituality of Fundraising* [The Henri Nouwen Spirituality Series] (Nashville, TN: Upper Room Books, 2010), 55.

Pastoring and Administering
a Mission-Driven Church

Jack Wall

I am certainly an anomaly in today's world—I was pastor of the same church for twenty-four years. That's Old St. Patrick's Church in Chicago, the oldest church structure in the city, dating back to 1856. It's located almost in the shadow of Sears Tower and right up against the interstate highway, making it a central city church. Like many urban churches in the Northeast part of our country, Old St. Pat's got its start serving the needs of Irish immigrants. It had a grammar school, two high schools, and several settlement houses, doing everything it could as a European immigrant Catholic Church. Over time, though, it evolved from a church of Irish immigrants to a church of Italian immigrants to a church of Mexican immigrants. When the interstate highway system was built in the early 1950s, it tore the neighborhood apart, forcing residents to move out in droves and triggering a dramatic drop in parish membership. When I became pastor in 1983, only four members remained in the entire parish.

When you think of a new parish forming today, it's often because hundreds of families converge on a suburban area. For me, it was a case of going into the center of a city and trying to start a church all over again after everyone had moved out. But believe it or not, that had tremendous appeal to me. I was always fascinated by the connectedness that's occurred throughout history between symbols and great dreams. For example, Martin Luther King went to the Lincoln Memorial to connect the country to its roots and to its deepest values and to preach "I've got a dream." When he became president, JFK went to Faneuil Hall in

Boston and unveiled his bold vision of a New Frontier. And if there's anything that our religion means to us today, I think it's that kind of connectedness. We reach back to the Scriptures and to the deep experiences of the divine in our humanity to build a new model for our faith.

And so, in taking over as pastor of Old St. Patrick's I had this profound sense of history, this connectedness, that working with others I could create a new type of church from this venerable but nearly abandoned inner-city shell. I learned a number of things along the way that I'd like to share.

First, I'll discuss a kind of foundational insight I had upon arriving at St. Pat's, then I'll describe how we committed ourselves to administrative excellence through a creative strategy I call Pastoring as Partnership. And finally, I'll turn my thoughts to what I think pastoring is about in the Catholic Church today, no matter where your parish is located or what constituents you serve.

Creating a Mission-Driven Church

My foundational insight flows from a hard fact of life when I took over at St. Pat's: we had a total of four members. I realized if we were going to start a church all over again, the way not to do it was to bring those four people together and ask them, "What are your needs?" I'm sure that's counterintuitive for most of us as pastors. Everything in our religious souls tells us to get people in the congregation together and ask them, "How can we serve you?"

But my insight was this: the church is not a member-centered institution. Clubs are member-centered institutions. The church is a *mission-driven* reality. That, of course, begs a very important question: what exactly is the mission of the church today, and, more specifically, what is its mission in the parish communities you're about to enter as new pastors?

To help answer that, let's take a closer look at the difference between member-centered and mission-driven. Member-centered institutions tout their privileges. The American Express Card has a well-known saying, "Membership has its privileges." And so often in parish life we get caught up in that kind of mind-set. "Are you a member?" "Members have privileges." Let me give you an example. The phone in the rectory rings. A secretary answers it and the young woman on the other end of the line says, "I just got engaged and would like to talk to you about holding my wedding at the church." What's the first question out of the secretary's mouth? "Are you a member?"

Consider, if we're saying to people, "You can't do this unless you're a member," then we've become a member-centered organization. And that shifts the focus completely when you think in terms of a church. The purpose of a church is clearly its mission. It's the reason people come to us. They believe in our mission and want to be part of it. They want to identify with the mission.

What I used to say to new members of St. Pat's was, "There are no privileges to being a member here, other than the new member's dinner when you join. From now on, this is about responsibility. How do we further the mission, the purpose, of the church, and how do we do it together?

Pastoring with Excellence

From my experiences at Old St. Patrick's, I've learned a number of things about leadership and administration. And the common thread among all of them, in a word, is "excellence." How do we pastor with excellence?

There's a wonderful business book on the subject of excellence that I think is also deeply spiritual. It's called *Good to Great* by Jim Collins, and it has relevance beyond just corporations. It explores how we can create excellent institutions that endure and prosper. What really caught my attention in this book is the opening line: "Good is the enemy of great."[1] What Collins seems to suggest is that excellence is within reach of all of us, but it requires us to go the extra mile, to think and act in ways that push us beyond our comfort level. Ways that propel us to excellence.

That challenge is germane to three changes I set in motion at St. Pat's that are all founded on the principle of what I call Pastoring as Partnership. The first change is especially important because one of the things we feel challenged by as pastors is how well we do as administrators. What helped me tremendously in the pursuit of excellent pastoring was the partnership I formed with a group of laypeople who served as a board of guarantors—not just a parish council but a board of guarantors that guaranteed the mission of Old St. Patrick's Church.

The board of guarantors is built on a platform as relevant to churches as it is to companies: sustainability. Your church is going to exist way beyond you. You're going to be pastor for awhile, then you're going to move on. But the dream of any good church must be to perpetuate its mission and its vision for decades, even centuries, to come. Old St. Patrick's, after all, has been around for more than 150 years.

Who's going to guarantee your mission into the future? I suggest you should be identifying a group of what I call "wisdom figures" that can help you look at the parish experience strategically, explore the key issues, and decide where you want to be at various points down the road—and certainly after you're gone. What are the dreams and the visions that will sustain the mission of your church?

That's the kind of direction I feel you should be taking through a partnership with an appointed board of guarantors. Not looking at all the practical things a pastoral council gets involved with, but focused instead on guaranteeing the mission of your church within the community for, hopefully, generations to come. In the case of Old St. Patrick's, having this core group of people who are always looking ahead, always looking strategically at where we want the mission of St. Pat's to track, was one of the great gifts that I received as pastor.

Find a Strong Business Partner

The second Pastoring as Partnership change I introduced involved a more focused and practical type of partnership. Let me try to put it in context. As St. Pat's began its new life, one of the things I would say to new staff members was, "I've got some good news and some bad news for you. First, the good news: this is a really exciting place to work. It's full of imagination and creativity and great energy. There are so many opportunities for you to exercise your gifts and talents. The bad news is: I'm your boss." And I said this very seriously to everybody because I don't consider myself a good manager at all. It's not my gift. I don't have strong management skills. I said this to new staff members for years, thinking all the time, "There's got to be a way to improve." Certainly, one way would have been to go out and personally develop those skills, but I really think there's a difference between leadership and management. Each calls for different skills. And upon reflection, I don't think one of the great gifts of a pastor is necessarily being a good manager, with all the requisite skills. But I think a pastor does have to be a leader. And leadership means being able to recognize and draw on the considerable benefits that emerge from partnerships.

Pastoring as Partnering

I became a true believer of this at Old St. Pat's when I managed to find a very strong business partner. He had retired early from a successful career and was looking for something to do in the nonprofit world. We connected and for the last thirteen years I was pastor he was my executive director, helping to manage not just the temporal side of the church but its mission on the formational side as well. He brought together our formational staff.

Many practitioners of pastoral ministry are not necessarily effective administrators of pastoral ministry. I tried to bridge that gap—and move closer to excellence—by tapping into this reservoir of highly skilled lay talent. I suggest to you that there are plenty of people out there who love the Catholic Church and want to serve it by offering their professional skills. I recognized this and used it to overcome my own shortcomings as an administrator by partnering with a man who happened to be a management genius.

As pastor, you're going to be given great responsibility and great authority under canon law to do this wonderful thing called pastoring. You're also going to be given great freedom to express yourself as a partner. You don't have to do it one way. You'll be able to use your imagination and creativity to do pastoring as excellently as you possibly can. And I strongly suggest that one thing you do as pastor with that authority is let others share that responsibility—and their gifts—with you.

Pope Benedict XVI said it beautifully in one of the first talks he gave to his priests in Rome. The pastor, he said, is not the only animator of the parish anymore. Pastors have to call on everybody to take responsibility for the mission of the church. As pastors, we're there to ensure that God's work gets done in the best way possible. And that means sharing the responsibilities you have with others who possess extraordinary gifts in fields like management and administration.

The Power of Joint Venturing

This brings me to the third leg of this pastoring–by–partnership approach: joint ventures. Not everything has to be built on a pyramid that has the pastor at the top doing it all, or the parish assuming sponsorship for everything you do. Let me give you an example based on my personal experience, which ties into the idea of a mission-driven church as well.

As we all know, Catholic schools are closing every day. And when that happens, private schools and charter schools rush in to rent their buildings as they expand their roles as educational entrepreneurs. That's exactly what happened at St. Pat's where our old facility was being rented to a private school. While pastor there, I became aware of a paradox: everybody wants to be in education, while the Catholic Church was backing away from it. I thought, "This is crazy. Why can't we do education like other entrepreneurs? There's a crying need for quality education in this city. Why don't we start a school?"

So, people from our congregation got together and after a lot of intense thought and discussion said, "Yes, we can do this. But let's do it practically." And so, we started a school with thirty-five kids—not in the school building we already had but in a storefront. And we started it not because our members needed it but because our church believed its mission in the central city could be powerfully expressed with a new kind of Catholic school. I'd like to emphasize this point. We were not a parochial school. A parochial school is meant to serve the members of the church. We started a Catholic school to serve the needs of the city. To be sure, it was deeply rooted in Catholic faith, but with a new kind of vision of what a school should look like in the center of the city. Today, the thirty-five original children have grown to eight hundred kids on two campuses as part of a flourishing Catholic enterprise in the heart of Chicago.

How does this relate to joint ventures? Because that's exactly what this imaginative school system is. We created a joint venture model—a separate 501(c)(3) organization that's part of the Archdiocese of Chicago. And because we wanted to do things that really addressed poverty in the city, we created a number of powerful social outreach programs, each a separate 501(c)(3). Significantly, the pastor or other members of our staff sit on the boards of these organizations. And now, a church that had a budget of under $100,000 when I came on board—and didn't even have funds for my salary—maintains a social outreach program in the neighborhood of $7 million. The budget for the school, by the way, is $15 million, though St. Pat's contribution to that is only about $350,000 a year.

So again, moving toward excellence meant adopting a new educational model for Old St. Patrick's. It meant creating joint ventures with other people and rejecting the notion of a member-centered school in favor of a mission-driven school that reached out in the spirit of our faith to everyone.

Let me recap my three suggestions as part of a Pastoring as Partnership initiative. First, name a board of guarantors that can take responsibility for the future vision and mission of your church. Second, get an administrative partner, somebody who loves the Catholic Church, has a strong management background, and can compensate for any management shortcomings you might have. And finally, don't think that everything in the parish has to emanate from you. There's a host of ways in which your mission can be expressed through a joint-venture model.

Expressing Our Faith through Communities

Continuing with the theme of mission-driven church, John Paul II wrote about the need to create experiences that move us into two different dimensions of reality.[2] One is *communio* and the other is *missio*. Within *communio*, the Eucharist, of course, is the most profound experience. But why is that so? Because it moves people to an awareness of being one in God. That is the deepest truth of every human being. It's the deepest truth of all things. We are one in God. Think of all the mystical language from St. John: "I am in you. You are in me. We are in God. God is in us."

Whatever the church does in terms of *communio*, it must be geared to creating experiences that deepen for people this awareness of their oneness in God, that move them to action because we believe God is a transforming God who heals and creates worlds of justice, compassion, and peace.

Think of all the things we're called to do in the two commandments, "Love God with all your heart, with all your soul, with all your being," and "Love your neighbor as yourself." *Communio* and *missio*: these embrace all the things we do when we create excellent experiences of church. And not just liturgy, which is such a powerful tool, but all the other faith-formational experiences where we invite people to a deeper awareness of the power of God's life and of God's spirit within them. We're really reaching for people's hearts, and the desire of your heart must be to put them in touch with the mystery of God's love and his grace and power and spirit.

One of the responsibilities that flows from *communio*, the mystery of life, is to create community. The problem is that community is always a mess, and parish is always a mess. But we have this sense of *communio* and this desire to create community. And what I suggest is that we work to create communities—plural—and not just a community. When St. Pat's started growing again—it now has about four thousand households—it was very obvious we couldn't be a community. But there were abundant opportunities for communities. And I think part of what we need to create in terms of the Catholic Church today is an opening to many types of communities. How do we strengthen the natural communities of family and friendship, the social communities of neighborhood? And how do we create faith communities, faith formational opportunities, retreat movements, youth movements, and all the things we express in that life of faith formation?

Toward a New Mission-Based Model

For me, one of the epochal movements in the history of the Catholic Church in America is now occurring. It's the Hispanicization of the church. All the demographics point to the fact that the future of the Catholic community in the United States is going to be non-European in its thrust. And you can't be an American Catholic today without being in touch with that experience.

Another epochal movement for the church is the new age of the *laos*, or the laity. Not laity as opposed to the clergy, but laity in terms of the people of God being called to go out and be transformative in the world. That movement is the incarnation of God's life and spirit and is something that we as a church ought to fully support. I'd like to suggest that one of the things that a church does in terms of *missio* is to find ways to send people into the world from their experience of communion. "Go, the Mass is ended."

How do we encourage and promote that mission-driven function within the Catholic Church? How do we move people from this experience of the divine into the world in which they live so they can be transformative? For most people, this opportunity will be realized by investing time and energy in worldly, secular institutions, like the corporation, the political party, the community organization, and within their own homes. But the church also creates expressions of justice and peace and compassion which, in turn, inspire people to create and bring ecclesial models of service into the world.

St. Pat's decided early on that it was going to try to eradicate poverty in the city of Chicago. And we settled on two ways of accomplishing that. One was traditional—using education to lift people out of poverty. The school we created has been very successful in doing that. But there are other programs in which our young adults are involved that are working hard to move inner-city people from poverty to opportunity. They include mentoring and helping them find jobs. One powerful program helps about two hundred homeless people a year get jobs, with benefits, and take responsibility for their lives. We also have missions in Central America, Latin America, Africa, and Asia where we touch the lives of others. When I think in terms of the age of the laity, I realize what we're trying to do is listen to the hearts of people who really love the church, love the gospel, and want to do God's work in the world.

How do we create a church model in which that energy, talent, creativity, and passion are unleashed? We can't do it through a top-down model. We have to break out of that traditional mold and realize that in the role of pastor we have this great opportunity to open up and unleash the energies of God's people in a way that really makes the Catholic Church a mission-driven forge. In sum, we must create experiences of church that help people deepen their sense of the presence and the mystery of their oneness with God. And with the gift of God's love and energy within them, they will choose to go out and live in mission to the world, *communio* and *missio*.

Endnotes

1. Jim Collins, *Good to Great: Why Some Companies Make the Leap . . . and Others Don't* (New York: HarperBusiness, 2001).

2. See Ralph Martin and Peter Williamson, eds., *John Paul II and the New Evangelization: How You Can Bring the Good News to Others* (Cincinnati: Servant Books, 2006).

10

Building Councils

Dennis Corcoran

In his book *The 360 Degree Leader*—which I highly recommend—John Maxwell made what I feel is a signature statement with respect to leadership.[1] He said that any organization will eventually take on the personality of its leader. I don't know what your experience has been, but I've found that every parish organization that I've been part of, including the one I grew up in, eventually took on the personality of the pastor. And that can be a very positive thing, or it can be a very scary thing.

So, my first insight today is *Know thyself, pastor!* Because if the organization is eventually going to take on your personality—whether you like it or not—you have to understand how you interact with people and the direction in which your personality leads you. How well does your personality take advice? Are you even open to advice, or are you the type whom Groucho Marx embraced when he said, "When I want your opinion, I'll beat it out of you. Until then, be quiet."

There are many different levels at which people take advice. Do you prefer advice in a group where you can process it within that setting? Or do you prefer advice one on one? How do you feel when people disagree with you? All of these variables are linked to your personality and will eventually be reflected in the organization. And when you think about that, it's kind of natural because people tend to want to please their leader, regardless of whether they like him or not. Therefore, they start to know how to act around that leader and, over time, will behave in a way that has the leader's stamp of approval.

You can see that very clearly in cases where there's been a change of pastor. Parishioners have, in a sense, been "trained" according to the personality of the prior pastor, and when his replacement comes on board exhibiting a new persona, people are at first uneasy. They don't know how to act because they're not clear what the new leadership is going to do. They don't yet know the personality of the pastor.

Gradually, though, the new pastor exerts his influence, and you can see the organization start to change. It starts to take on the personality of its leader. That's why it's so important if you're a pastor, or about to become a pastor, to think about how the organization is going to be influenced by your personality and your leadership skills. If you truly know yourself, you'll be better able to build effective councils and staffs that can advise you within your comfort zone. Trying to do it any other way could be very difficult for you and for the parish.

The Birth of Parish Councils

A natural place to start our discussion on council building is the Second Vatican Council, which called for the creation of parish councils. The decree of the Apostolate of the Laity says, "In dioceses, insofar as possible, there should be councils which assist the apostolic work of the Church either in the field of evangelization and sanctification or in the charitable, social, or other spheres, and here it is fitting that the clergy and Religious should cooperate with the laity. While preserving the proper character and autonomy of each organization, these councils will be able to promote the mutual coordination of various lay associations and enterprises. Councils of this type should be established as far as possible also on the parochial, interparochial, and interdiocesan level as well as in the national or international sphere" (26).[2]

So, while Vatican II established councils at the diocesan level, it recommended that whenever possible, they be mirrored at the parish level too. More than forty years later, the most effective councils I'm aware of at both levels are referred to as "pastoral councils." Indeed, I want very much to help you understand the difference between a parish/pastoral council and a finance council.

Let's move from the language of the Apostolate of the Laity (1965) to the Code of Canon Law (1983): "If the diocesan bishop judges it opportune after he has heard the presbyteral council, a pastoral council is to be established in each parish, over which the pastor presides and in which the Christian faithful, together with those who share in pastoral care by virtue of their office in the parish"—in other words, laypeople like myself—"assist in fostering pastoral activity" (c. 536 §1). Further, "A pastoral council possesses a consultative vote only"—consultative *voice* would be a better way of saying this—"and is governed by the norms established by the diocesan bishop" (c. 536 §2).

You can see from the language of both these documents that parish councils are a recommended approach to parish leadership—but they are not mandatory. I wouldn't suggest that you not have one, but the truth of the matter is they're not mandated.

Finance Councils Are Mandated

The Second Vatican Council also called for the creation of parish finance councils.

The Code of Canon Law reads: "In each parish, there is to be a finance council which is governed, in addition to universal law"—which means it's part of universal law and therefore can't be dismissed by the diocesan bishop—"by norms issued by the diocesan bishop and in which the Christian faithful, selected according to these same norms, are to assist the pastor in the administration of the goods of the parish, without prejudice to the prescript of can. 532" (c. 537).

Notice the difference in official language between the creation of parish councils and finance councils. Finance councils are mandated. Every parish needs to have one and most dioceses, if not all, have developed policies around those bodies that dictate, among other things, how to prepare and submit budgets and have them signed by the appropriate people.

Based on my experience over the years as pastoral associate and director of operations at Presentation Church [in Upper Saddle River, New Jersey] and Church of Christ the King [in New Vernon, New Jersey], I feel strongly that both councils must be rooted in mission and prayer. There has to be some sort of a mission and some sort of a vision of where the parish is headed, and they need to be rooted in a shared prayer at the beginning of each parish council or finance council meeting. I feel very strongly about the opening prayer. Because it sets a positive tone for the rest of the meeting, it needs to be well thought out by you or someone you delegate. And it needs to be brought forth in a way that aids the discussion and whatever else might be on the agenda.

On the subject of prayer, I highly recommend retreat days for both parish and finance council members. Bring in a facilitator from the outside to run a Saturday morning program that's just spiritual in nature. I can't emphasize that enough because it's important to have councils that are rooted not just in business but, even more important, in prayer.

Selecting Members

Who should you have on your councils? Let me answer that by using a line from Jim Collins's excellent book, *Good to Great*: "It's not so much who's on the bus, but who needs to get off."[3] Let me restate that absolutely marvelous piece of advice: worry about who shouldn't be on the bus rather than about filling all the seats.

You don't want someone who's antagonistic and a constant thorn in your side—someone who's forever marching in the opposite direction. At the same time, you don't want a bunch of "yes" people who rubber-stamp everything you say. Who you want on your councils are people who have strong opinions but can respectfully disagree. You want people who can continue with the mission even if you or the group decides to move in another direction.

Make variety the hallmark of your council membership. Be sure different age groups are represented—including men and women—and that they reflect varied lengths of time in the parish. Don't always assume that the best people are those who have been in the parish the longest. Some of the best people may be new arrivals with the ability to see the parish through a fresh set of eyes. At my own parish, we have people who are new to the congregation as well as founding members on our pastoral council. And as we've seen time and again, that composition makes for wonderful advice, feedback, and interaction.

With the right types of people, you can create positive energy around council meetings. If it's painful for you and everyone else to hold those meetings, then you probably shouldn't. To avoid that kind of dead end, you need to determine in advance what positive outcomes you want to emerge from the meeting, then focus your energy and passion on making them happen. If *you're* not passionate about the wonderful things that can flow from your pastoral or finance council, then it's going to come across to members and set a negative tone for any proceedings. I can't stress enough the urgency of finding a reason why your next council meeting is important to you and parish members.

Appointed vs. Elected Members

In addition, I'd like to advise against having a voting process within the parish for selecting council members. The reason is, it's too dangerous. Since you have no idea as pastor who's going to be joining the council, you lose control over who "needs to be on the bus" and who doesn't. Instead, I firmly believe that all members should be invited by you to serve on the councils. Simply put, they should be pastoral appointments.

I see that practice rooted in the mission of Christ, quite honestly. At no point do we see in the Scriptures that Jesus invited all the disciples together and said, "Okay, let's vote on the final twelve." Instead, he approached a varied group of people and deliberately said, "Come, follow me." It was really a personal invitation in which he told his disciples, "I need your help. Come, join in the mission."

Just to reiterate, you want on your leadership councils people who can bring something to the table, people who are good at giving advice. To that end, I encourage you to get input from outgoing members and staff before making an appointment. On any staff that I've been part of, when council terms were about up, the pastor would sit down with his people and say, "Recommendations, anybody?" That was an opportunity for him in effect to declare, "Here's who I'm thinking of. What do you think?"

Helpful Rules of the Road

There certainly has to be term limits for council members. Nobody wants to serve on a parish council if they think it might be a life sentence. You'll get a much better response if you ask someone for a finite amount of time. From what I've seen, two- or three-year terms with a renewable term work best. If a person has done really valuable work and both of you are excited about his or her presence on the council, you should be able to renew the person for another two years. That way, the most anyone would spend on a council is five years. After serving five years, the person would have to take at least a year off—some parishes require two years—before he or she could be invited back.

What's more, I don't recommend having ministry leaders on the parish council. The reason is, there's a natural urge on their part to push the agenda of their ministry. It's therefore a bit of a conflict of interest for them to sit on a council which hopefully is taking an objective view of issues that come before it. Clearly, it's much healthier if a council member is not the point person for a ministry. All council members at our parish are involved in ministry, of course, but none of them are the ministry leaders. So, if they want to be on the council, or if we invite them to be on the council, we ask them to spend the next three months finding their replacements in their specific ministries.

One of the things that we do at Church of Christ the King—which is a smaller parish—is that the pastor or I personally meet with every new family that's registering in the parish. This allows them to get to know the parish leadership, which should make them a little more comfortable. Just as important, though, it gives us a chance to find out what *their* strengths and talents are and what they do for a living. Through this welcoming process we may learn, for example, that a new parish member is a CPA, or someone who practices nonprofit law, and realize they would be a perfect addition to our finance council when someone's term is up. We might also find out that someone has experience in strategic planning, and we realize the person would be an excellent fit for our pastoral council.

So again, effective council management is about vision and mission. It's about building a parish that everyone can be proud of and that everyone can feel great about. And the keeper of that vision is the pastor.

There's an unwritten rule that you should leave everything alone for at least one year after taking over as pastor. I agree with that concept. However, it's also advisable to have constant dialogue and evaluation over that period where you share your opinion and others share theirs, and where you offer suggestions about how things might be done differently the following year. Certainly, if you have a direction or a plan that you believe is going to work better for you and the parish in terms of building and managing the leadership councils, then I would encourage you to actively pursue it from the very beginning. You have to recognize that not everyone is going to like what you're doing. But hopefully a majority of people *will* like your direction and vision as parish leader. Personally, if I was forced to choose, I would rather have on my tombstone "He was well-respected" than "He was well-liked."

The Role of Subcommittees

Nor should you be afraid of forming subcommittees and task forces. Don't think that everything has to be done at council meetings. In fact, if your meetings are lasting more than an hour-and-a-half or two hours, you're probably doing something wrong. What I've found helpful in our parish is that if an item is on the table and we don't have all the information in front of us that we need, I say to the group, "Let's have a subcommittee figure this out," or "Let's create a task force to handle it." Either the pastor or I then charge those members with getting the information they need and coming back with a recommendation that the full council can act on at the next meeting.

Obviously, I'm a big fan of off-loading work to subcommittees and task forces at almost every meeting we have. Rather than have a 45-minute discussion on an issue that's going nowhere, tap two or three people from the meeting who will agree to meet at another time. It works wonderfully in terms of moving along the agenda.

Pros and Cons of Discernment

I'm a big fan of discernment in general, and if you have the time and the resolve to use it for your councils, it could work well. After you have your nominees, invite them to an evening of prayer and share with them your vision and what stage you're at in your pastorate. Describe to them the goals of the parish and those areas you plan on making your priorities. And once you've explained all that, get their input and ask them to complete a form with entries, such as, "I feel I could be of value to the council in the following ways" and "I would bring the following skills and expertise to the council."

The one concern I have with some discernment processes is that they take up substantial Mass time during the two or three Sundays when you're trying to make the nomination process fair and upfront. They then require additional time for meetings, prayers, and the like. So, there's a lot of effort involved, but if you feel you're going to get a more favorable result than you would from appointing council members, and you're passionate about it, then I certainly wouldn't discourage you from pursuing it.

The Right Size Council

What's the ideal size for a parish or finance council? When I was a communication studies major, a small group was described as three to seven people. Well, a parish council should not be looked upon as a small group. While there are no hard and fast rules, a council probably shouldn't consist of more than twelve people if you're looking for a manageable group for discussion purposes. After all, we had the twelve apostles, so that seems to be the optimal number.

Questions sometimes arise, too, over council membership in a multicultural parish.

My advice here is to look for that individual who is the natural, organic leader within the cultural or ethnic group and have a conversation with the person to get valuable input. It's helpful to ask this person, "Who are the best folks to have on our pastoral council in terms of not only representing your cultural group but also in helping to advance the overall vision of the parish?"

In the Florida parish I was a member of, we had probably four different cultural groups, and each had at least one representative on the parish council. We worked very hard to pull all these individuals together, and because they all were natural leaders, they had the respect of the entire congregation.

Resources to Guide You

To help guide you through questions and issues like these, I highly recommend a book called *Revisioning the Parish Pastoral Council: A Workbook*.[4] It's terrific in terms of describing how to work with diverse groups in your parish in order to get to a specific mission and vision—and eventually to those people who will serve effectively on the council.

Another book that's been really helpful to me—and which I feel is indispensable to you as pastors—is *The Pastoral Companion: A Canon Law Handbook for Catholic Ministry* by John Huels.[5] This marvelous document gives you all the canons, sorted by topic, and interpretations of each. It's an outstanding resource and reference tool that can save you many calls to the chancery every time you have a procedural question.

Parish finance councils also benefit from some excellent resource materials. One is a pamphlet put out by the National Leadership

Roundtable called *A Parishioner's Guide to Parish Finances*. It poses fifteen questions that people need to ask about their parish's finances. For example: Does my parish have a finance council? Does my parish finance council meet regularly and do its members have professional backgrounds? Does my parish finance council publish an annual budget, and are parish officials available to discuss it?[6]

Canon law, by the way, mandates publishing the parish budget for parishioners. At Church of Christ the King, we've gone a step further. Our leadership councils publish an annual report that tells parishioners what our goals are, where the money went over the past year, and what we hope to accomplish going forward. And we do that in a narrative form that's clear and comprehensible for most people.

Another critical document for any parish finance council is a charter. It's particularly useful for new council members when they join so they can see what their mission is, how the body operates, and what their duties are as members. In our parish we took the charter from our diocese and used it as a model to draw up our own finance council charter.

Spotlighting Council Members

My last recommendation for both finance and pastoral councils has a public relations touch. I suggest giving members of these councils some well-deserved recognition and exposure by highlighting them in your parish bulletin or website. We do that through question-and-answer interviews with council members—conducted by a parishioner—which we then publish along with their pictures. This way people get to know the members and their backgrounds and are in a better position to ask questions or offer advice.

As part of that effort, it's really useful to identify people in the parish with writing or journalism skills who can write such items for your bulletin or website. As pastors, don't be afraid during Mass to issue an appeal for help. You'll probably be surprised at the positive response you get.

Endnotes

1. John C. Maxwell, *The 360 Degree Leader: Developing Your Influence from Anywhere in the Organization* (Nashville, TN: Nelson Books, 2005).

2. Second Vatican Council, *Apostolicam Actuositatem* (Decree on the Apostolate of the Laity), 1965.

3. Jim Collins, *Good to Great: Why Some Companies Make the Leap . . . and Others Don't* (New York: HarperBusiness, 2001).

4. Mary Ann Gubish, Susan Jenny, and Arlene McGannon, *Revisioning the Parish Pastoral Council: A Workbook* (Mahwah, NJ: Paulist Press, 2001).

5. John M. Huels, *The Pastoral Companion: A Canon Law Handbook for Catholic Ministry*, 4th updated ed. (Montreal: Wilson & Lafleur, 2009).

6. National Leadership Roundtable on Church Management, *A Parishioner's Guide to Parish Finances*. A free copy is available at: www.theleadershiproundtable .org/TLR/documents/Parishioners_Guide_to_Understanding_Parish_Finances .pdf.

Standards for Excellence

Michael Brough

There's no end today to the burdensome issues that can keep a pastor awake at night. They include finances, hiring and firing, school closings, planning, stewardship, evangelization, mission, and fundraising, to name just a few. It seems the more dynamic the parish, the more intense the issues with which you and your parish must contend.

My goal is to explore with you some tools and resources that can help you address these issues in a practical, focused, and effective way. They fall into the categories of accountability, performance indicators, and benchmarks.

As for the first of those tools, it's interesting how the word "accountability" is now coming to the fore within the U.S. Catholic Church. In my travels, I've heard many experienced priests say, "Well, I've talked about it for years, but now we're finally *doing* something." There now seems to be a realization by everyone of the role accountability must play if we're going to achieve meaningful change within the church.

The challenge, however, is this: "accountability," like "stewardship" and "collaborative ministry," is this beautiful word that sits out there and prompts us to say, "That's a great idea. We should try to do it." But that begs a couple of pointed questions: what processes must be in place for us to say we're an accountable parish, and how does accountability actually take place?

When I think of the second tool, performance indicators, I recall the famous throwaway line by the late New York City Mayor Ed Koch when he was out on the streets, "How am I doing?" As a pastor, how do you know how well *you're* doing? Sometimes a staff member, parishioner or the bishop will give you constructive feedback. But experience shows there is no more reliable and effective a tool than performance indicators. They allow you to honestly and accurately say, "This is how well, or poorly, I'm doing. These are the natural skills and gifts I have. Here are areas that are difficult for me and for which I should be getting outside help."

And finally, benchmarks. How do you bring objectivity to the complex process of managing a parish? If you can establish benchmarks and be able to say, "Here is what a well-run parish looks like, here is what effective stewardship looks like, and here is what good human resources management looks like," then you have some powerful standards by which to judge the performance of your parish and its people.

Spirituality of Leadership

The philosopher and teacher Jean Vanier had some marvelous thoughts about the spirituality of leadership. He said, "Leaders of communities need to *organize* the community so that each member is in the right place and things work smoothly. They need to *animate* it, so that it continues to be alive and the eyes of all are fixed on the essential goals. They need to *love* each person and be concerned about their growth."[1]

That quote reminds me that you can't separate the pastoral leader from the organizer and from the animator of the parish. If we're talking about implementing solutions to some of the difficult issues you face as pastors, then the idea that we need to organize and animate and love each person and be concerned about their growth takes on tremendous relevance. Indeed, if that's your approach to pastoring, then you're already blessed with a spirituality of leadership, and that separates you from others who are saddled with a need to do things a certain way because that's how they've always been done.

It's been my experience that virtually every priest, when confronted with a major issue, will take the position, "I want to be the best priest I can be for my parish and for the spiritual growth of my people. That's why I'm doing what I'm doing." I'm not suggesting you have to be a financial, human resources, or administrative expert to be successful in your roles. But to be the "best priest" you do need to know enough about these complex areas to make sure they're being efficiently managed, and that you're being an effective organizer and animator of your parish.

Let's be honest. You weren't ordained to grapple with many of these temporal issues, and as priests and pastors you often find yourselves sidetracked. But I can assure you, there are processes, procedures, policies, approaches, and structures you can put in place to ensure that those sidetracks happen less frequently. The reason for that is, you'll have the right people with the right plan in the right place. And when that happens, a potent chemistry is unleashed that will allow you as pastor to fulfill your ministry at a variety of levels, not the least of which is taking care of the administration of your parish. The final goal, of course, is not to be great managers for the sake of being great managers. It's how we can be effective in our mission as a parish and how *you* can be the best pastoral leader you possibly can.

The Need for an Ethics/Accountability Code

With those objectives in mind, the National Leadership Roundtable on Church Management put together the *Standards for Excellence: An Ethics and Accountability Code for Catholic Parishes, Dioceses and Nonprofits*.[2] We realized there was so much to cover that having it all in one place, as a simple and convenient resource for people, would be extremely helpful.

Consider the first word of the title: "Standards." We want you to know there's a right way to do things—and it doesn't mean the bare minimum. To be sure, canon law proscribes what you can and can't do as a pastor. But it's not just internal rules you have to be concerned about. Civil laws also dictate what you can and can't do. If you stray, outside agencies will be only too happy to come in and remind you that you have legal responsibilities; that you can't, for example, fire someone simply because they're "too old." There are rules and practices we have to live by, and we've encapsulated many of them in our *Standards for Excellence*.

When you look at the Catholic Church today, it's clear there are plenty of ethical issues that result in clashes between right and wrong behavior, right and wrong practices, and right and wrong policies. Needless to say, we haven't always gotten things right, which underscores the need for an ethics and accountability code. And while we based ours on a not dissimilar code from the secular, nonprofit sector, we customized the *Standards for Excellence* specifically to the needs of the Catholic Church and brought them into conformity with canon law.

I should point out that accountability is not an alien concept within the church. I refer you to the U.S. Bishops' Pastoral Letter on Stewardship in 1993. It states that accountability is a fundamental concept linked to our Christian understanding of stewardship, and that we need to "render an account of the organization's use of the time, talent, and treasure entrusted to its care." And in a line that sounds like it's straight from a Wall Street advisor, the bishops' letter concludes, "As the demand for charitable giving grows (and competition increases), accountability will become an even more important indicator of whether an organization is 'worthy of investment.' "[3]

So, accountability needs to be central in meeting the spiritual, educational, and social needs of the people you are called on to serve. Again, this is not an alien concept. Nor does it involve some vague notion because in that same letter the bishops maintain that good stewardship as it relates to church finances needs to have stringent ethical, legal, and fiscal standards. They couldn't be clearer that sound business practice needs to be an integral part of how we run our parishes.

In order to customize best practices for the church, the challenge is often one of language and translation. We are frequently talking about the same thing, just using different terminology or jargon. It is not "corporate" to say, "Do you want to be the best DRE you can be? Do you want to know what you're being asked to do? Do you want to be able to measure how well you're doing it?"

Standards for Excellence, for its part, covers some fifty-five performance benchmarks that offer a comprehensive blueprint for a well-managed and responsibly run Catholic parish. In short, it's a model by which parishes can implement ethical standards and accountability practices. *Standards for Excellence* doesn't try to dictate how you implement every last detail. But it does attempt to ensure that you have all important bases covered and, just as important, that you have the framework for an enduring code of best practices within your parish.

When we put together the *Standards for Excellence*, we had to make sure they were 100 percent in conformance with canon law. Our canon lawyers assured us that not only were they in total conformance, but they even strengthened canon law because they were more explicit about how to fulfill your responsibilities under church rules.

Eight Guiding Principles

With that as background, what does *Standards for Excellence* cover? There are eight guiding principles, or drivers, for the fifty-five benchmarks we cover, beginning with mission and program. In other words, why are we doing what we're doing? What *is* our mission, and how do our activities in the parish help promote that?

Second is governance and advisory bodies, like finance and pastoral councils and, at the diocesan level, presbyteral councils and diocesan finance councils.

The third guiding principle revolves around conflicts of interest. This has proven to be quite an interesting area because as I go around the country, I find it an issue that people have intensely debated but rarely done anything about, except on a one-off basis. Yet it's amazing the number of problems that arise in parishes that can be traced back to conflicts of interest. Few people realize how relatively simple it is to resolve them.

The fourth guiding principle is human resources. This is a huge area that covers everything from hiring and firing to how you develop and help people to grow in their jobs and their vocations. Is there a difference between the two? For my generation, there certainly isn't. My job in the church *is* a vocation—it's what I've been called to do. So the question becomes how, within human resources, do we help people to grow in their jobs and better serve the church?

The remaining guiding principles center on financial and legal responsibilities; openness, which gets back to the transparency issue; fundraising; and public policy and public affairs.

Implementing the Standards

How do we go about applying best practices incorporated in *Standards for Excellence* in each of these areas? And, just as importantly, how do we make them sustainable?

The good news is, we're not talking about reinventing the wheel. We're talking about tapping into best practices that already exist in the corporate, nonprofit, and secular worlds, and even within other parishes and dioceses. The challenge, though, is weaving them into the fabric of the parish. And that will require nothing short of a culture change that looks to your leadership skills and your ability to engage your staff, lay leaders, and the entire parish in a meaningful conversation. Learning how to be agents of change and how to manage sweeping change across your parishes is a powerful leadership skill for you to develop. How do you help people recognize that "our situation is different now than it was before" and that we need to change accordingly if we're going to continue to be effective in our ministry?

In order to implement a *Standards for Excellence* program, you'll need a champion. That can be you, a pastoral associate, the parochial vicar, the head of your pastoral council, or a lay leader. Maybe the person doesn't even have a title, but you know he or she is the leader within the community.

Once you've identified a champion, you need to determine the folks you should be in dialogue with, and how you want to share this common value that says you want to integrate standards for excellence into the way you do things because you believe it will result in the best parish you can possibly be going forward. The most important message that needs to be conveyed to your people is that you have a mission, and you have a vision, and you're putting in place the building blocks—the standards for excellence—to get you there.

So, you begin with a self-assessment. This is really about you and your people looking at your parish and recognizing which areas you're managing well and identifying others that you need to focus on and improve, either through quick fixes or long-term programs. As the next step, we at the Leadership Roundtable provide you with the tools you need—like education resources, templates, case studies, and policy manuals—for a successful implementation.

Another message is that as a church, we need to take the areas of accountability and ethics very seriously. This involves professionalizing our church leadership and also coming to the realization that prevention is better than the cure. And it's not just the Leadership Roundtable preaching this. When Bishop Dennis Schnurr, now Archbishop Schnurr, was treasurer of the Bishops Conference, he said, "Our parishes can no longer be mom–and–pop businesses with 'trust me' as their motto."[4]

That's not to question the integrity of your bookkeeper, your collection counter, your accountant, your finance council chair, or you as pastor. Rather, one of the benefits of standards for excellence is that these key individuals are actually protected. Why would you want to put any of your lay volunteers or staff members into a situation where there are no checks and balances to safeguard them? Even if you're able as pastor to transfer a lot of parish responsibilities to talented and qualified laypeople, that doesn't let you off the hook either. Checks and balances protect everyone.

Protecting and professionalizing your parish also means plugging into your diocese. Many dioceses have developed policies and procedures to protect you and other parish leaders. But no small number of dioceses I work with have told me their biggest challenge is moving from development of the policy to its implementation—and that takes us back to the issue of accountability. Diocesan policies are usually explained in huge binders, so it's not surprising that people often don't look at them. But what we also frequently find is that nowhere in the development of these policies and procedures did the diocese involve lay leaders at the parish level. My advice to you is, don't make the same mistake with respect to standards for excellence. If you don't involve your folks in the development and implementation of these benchmarks, then don't expect buy-in and a sense of ownership down the line. It's really about entering into a dialogue with your people and saying to them, "Here's why we see the need for this particular policy or procedure, and because of your expertise we'd like you to help us develop it for the sake of the parish."

Tackling Tough Issues

Once the standards have been implemented, what are some specific issues they can help you address in a professional and responsible manner?

Let's take the area of conflicts of interest. While one approach to avoiding conflicts is to recuse yourself from serving on a council or committee if there appears to be a conflict, we all know that seldom works in parishes. This brings us to a far more effective approach—transparency—that's inherent in *Standards for Excellence*. Every year, members of your pastoral council and finance council openly state, "Here are the relationships that I have." Maybe the car dealer who gave you a break on your Buick also serves on the finance council. Or maybe the local small business owner who's supplying your parish school with its stationery also serves on your pastoral council and votes on the budget. Transparency throws the spotlight on these relationships and opens the door for people to proactively say, "Here is when I must recuse myself from a decision on a particular matter."

There's another way the standards can help. Do you have a confidential process by which people can report improprieties? This became a major issue for the church with the sexual abuse crisis. Do you or your diocese have a hotline to report financial irregularities? As pastor, you certainly want to be sure you have this capability. It gets back to what I said before about protecting your parish and your people. If you have the proper policies and procedures in place, if your finance council is meeting regularly, if you're confident that your annual report, your budget, and the information you give to your parishioners is accurate, then you have nothing to fear.

Like conflicts of interest, performance evaluation is a critical area that very few parishes seem to handle well. The standards for excellence provide for measuring the performance of your staff members against a predetermined set of goals and expectations, and using that information to strengthen the staff's skills, productivity, and job satisfaction. The performance evaluation process helps to generate an ongoing dialogue with your people so that an underperforming head of a ministry, for example, might feel comfortable approaching you to say, "It's obviously not working out. You're looking for me to do X and Y, but I can't seem to raise myself to those levels. I probably need to be elsewhere."

So now the conversation on your part becomes, how can I help you find the right place for your talents? Perhaps the right place is still on staff but in a different role. Or perhaps it's in another parish at a different stage of its development that needs precisely the skills you have to offer. What you're showing that person is that you care enough to help him or her transition to something that better meets that person's needs. And this is especially important since our pastoral staff and volunteers are not simply "employees" but often parishioners, friends, and part of a wider family of faith.

Term limits is another example of how the standards can provide valuable guidance. You may have people who have served on your pastoral council for twenty or thirty years. That's wonderful, but you need to get them off—not a permanent leave, they can come back in two or three years, say—but you need an infusion of fresh ideas from new members on your councils. These new individuals may have been sitting on the sidelines for years, waiting for an opportunity to serve the parish.

Standards can also impact council and staff development. How do you orient new members of your pastoral and finance councils? Do you insist that they attend diocesan training sessions on subjects of interest? Do you encourage them to take, and perhaps provide funding for, courses at a local college or seminary? All of these can be very worthwhile investments.

Mentoring is important. I wouldn't be standing here today if it weren't for mentors, many of them priests. Whatever you call it— mentoring, professional coaching, leadership development, or pastoral care—the process is vital. It answers the questions, "How are you helping me to grow as an individual?" And "How are you helping your staff to convincingly address the questions and issues they face?"

Online Resources

Beyond *Standards for Excellence*, there are two online resources available to help your parish become more dynamic and enable you to step back from the extraordinary demands of running a modern-day parish and develop thoughtful processes and structures that are linked to the mission of your parish.[5] Very few priests today have the luxury of taking time to travel for courses, sabbaticals, or other extended learning opportunities. In some dioceses, there are very few opportunities for ongoing formation. So imagine, then, a site where you can go to get the latest insights and thinking in key ministry areas like liturgies, sacramental life, prayer life for parishioners, communication, council effectiveness, or for any other topic you'd like to bring to the forum and initiate a discussion. Or a site where you can find out about upcoming national conferences, notable speeches and remarks, and published articles on subjects of interest to you. All of these are available within a shared community of practice—your fellow priests and pastors.

CatholicPastor.org

In response to needs identified by priests in Leadership Roundtable programs like the Toolbox for Pastoral Management, a protected online space created by priests, run by priests, and used exclusively by priests, was established. CatholicPastor.org is a web-based learning community that empowers Catholic priests to engage in an extended conversation and learn from one another across a range of spiritual, pastoral, and administrative responsibilities. This community of practice offers a comprehensive approach to clergy support and development through the opportunity to contribute experiences and practical resources in discussion forums and find helpful content in a digital resource center.

Online forums and networks have significantly reduced the time and space needed to learn how to respond to the challenges one may face as the spiritual, pastoral, and administrative leader of a parish. As we all know, the experience can be overwhelming, and the apprenticeship period leading up to it is often non-existent. Over 600 priests from across the country use this online venue to share best practices with one another. It aims to highlight what works well in some parishes and then distribute those solutions nationally for implementation in other parishes.

Catholicstandardsforum.org

The Catholic Standards for Excellence Forum is an online resource of best financial, human resources, communications, and management practices for use in Catholic parishes. Additionally, this free resource serves as an online gathering place for diocesan, parish, and Catholic nonprofit professionals to share best practices, engage in problem-solving conversation, and craft solutions in a collaborative, safe space. With fewer opportunities for travel and professional development opportunities, the Catholic Standards for Excellence Forum provides you and your pastoral leadership team and volunteers cost-effective solutions to collaborate, learn best practices, and share ideas.

Developing Leadership Skills

Finally, I'd like to mention *Catholic Leadership 360*, a 360-degree leadership assessment for priests.[6] This joint effort of the National Federation of Priests' Councils, the National Association of Church Personnel Administrators, and the National Leadership Roundtable on Church Management is designed to give you feedback on your ministerial leadership effectiveness. This feedback comes from your superior, your peers, those in ministry with you, and those you minister to. It can be a very affirming process that also assists you in your development as a pastoral leader. It enables you to analyze your results and create a development plan that's aligned with your parish or diocesan plan or strategy.

The *360-Degree Leadership Assessment* is confidential. The only person who receives your report is you. Not the bishop. Not the vicar general. Not the head of clergy personnel. But I believe you'll find this tool so helpful that you'll be prompted to go to your bishop and your head of personnel afterward and say, "Here's my personal development plan. These are my strengths, and these are areas I know I need to work on."

Like the other programs I've described, *360-Degree Leadership Assessment* is based on proven best practices in the corporate, nonprofit, and secular worlds and customized for a church context. In your case, the Assessment Tool for Priests follows the exhortation of *Pastores Dabo Vobis*, the *Basic Plan for the Ongoing Formation of Priests*, and specific resources like *In Fulfillment of Their Mission: The Duties and Tasks of a Roman Catholic Priest.*[7]

Taken together, these tools give you a powerful resource to help you learn from your experiences and share that knowledge with your brother pastors and priests. There's no better way to send you on a lifelong journey of personal growth, formation, theological education, and human development—a journey whose end point is excellence for you and your parish.

Endnotes

1. See Jean Vanier, *Community and Growth*, rev. ed. (Mahwah, NJ: Paulist Press, 1989), 208.

2. National Leadership Roundtable on Church Management, *Standards for Excellence: An Ethics and Accountability Code for Catholic Parishes* (2007), www.CatholicStandardsForExcellence.org.

3. USCCB, *Stewardship: A Disciple's Response* (Washington, DC: USCCB Publishing, 2002), 63.

4. Archbishop Dennis M. Schnurr, "Lead Us Not into Temptation," *National Catholic Reporter* 43, no. 14 (February 2, 2007): 19.

5. All resources can be accessed at TheLeadershipRoundtable.org.

6. Visit www.CatholicLeadership360.org.

7. John Paul II, Apostolic Exhortation, *Pastores Dabo Vobis* (25 March 1992); USCCB, *Basic Plan for the Ongoing Formation of Priests* (Washington, DC: USCCB Publishing, 2001); Joseph Ippolito, Mark Latcovich, and Joyce Malyn-Smith, *In Fulfillment of Their Mission: The Duties and Tasks of a Roman Catholic Priest* (Washington, DC: National Catholic Educational Assocation, 2008).

Parish Planning

Jim Lundholm-Eades

Planning in a Catholic parish setting is about strengthening *communio* and aligning around a common purpose: *missio*. A parish plan is an agreement within the *communio* about how to go about its *missio*—about reading the signs of the times, deciding what is important at this time, when to do what for how long, and how to know when progress is being made. Most high-level (sometimes called "strategic") planning is documented. It is mission-driven, data-informed and discernment-derived. In a Catholic parish setting a defined planning process is important, and how planning happens should in itself enhance the experience of *communio* and highlight the focus on *missio*.

Good parish planning is a relational activity. In fact, a pastoral plan for the parish ultimately consists of relationships themselves, not the written document. The written planning document only records for the purpose of future reference the basis for the relationships between the people involved in the planning process. It records why this community called a parish gathers (mission), what it will look like when this group is living in accord with their reason for existence (vision), what this community agreed to do (priorities), how they agreed to go about it (strategies), and who is accountable to whom, for what and by when. How the parish goes about planning is, therefore, far more important than the written plan itself.

It is important to realize from the beginning that planning is not, in itself, rocket science. In fact, keeping it simple and straightforward is essential. This chapter provides a Catholic parish a pragmatic, step-by-step guide through the planning process.

Why Plan?

Planning in a parish helps create mission focus and alignment from the governance level through to the operational level within the parish. A parish planning process has a clearly defined end. It gives the parish a roadmap for the near term and midterm future. It tells the parish leadership and community its priorities for the next two to three years and helps them keep a long-term context in mind. The planning process begins with catechesis that teaches the community about the mission of the church universal and moves from there to clarify the mission of the diocese and the parish. It articulates the vision and near-term priorities of the parish, offering a roadmap of what needs to be done in the next two to three years to bring the parish closer to making its mission and vision a reality. The plan itself gives the pastor, lay leadership, administrative structure, and community of the parish a basis for making decisions about how it organizes its resources. At its best, the planning process is itself an experience of robust *communio* that strengthens the ongoing experience of *communio* and the focus on *missio*.

Adaptive vs. Predictive Planning

After World War II, strategic planning was introduced to businesses and parishes through the experience of those who had been in the military. In the 1960s and 1970s, strategic planning was seen as the "silver bullet" for success. During the 1980s, many were disenchanted with strategic planning in parishes until they realized that much of what had passed for strategic planning erroneously presumed that the conditions under which a plan was created were predictable and largely static, resulting in a document that sat gathering dust on a shelf. It was out of that experience that adaptive planning was born. This approach assumed that both internal and external operating environments for a parish shift continuously and so any useful plan would be one that continuously adapts. Parish planning today, then, has gone beyond the static "five-year plan" model to an adaptive and creative process integrated into parish life. Adaptive planning recognizes that many of the factors influencing parish life such as demographic change, economic conditions in the local and wider community, changes to employment regulations, shifts in the expectations of donors, and expectations about fiscal transparency and accountability are beyond the control of the parish and are becoming less than predictable. Adaptive planning allows the parish to more effectively live its mission within a changing internal and external environment.

Understanding the Broad Strokes of Parish Planning

The best parish planning processes are mission-driven, data-informed, and discernment-derived. This means that good planning begins with catechesis of parish leadership and those who will have a direct role in the planning process, as well as the wider parish community. The use of the word catechesis here is important. It is a breaking open of the mission given to the church by Jesus using scripture and other documents or literature from the Catholic tradition. In the past this meant just writing a mission statement. What is being suggested here is much deeper.

It begins with formative catechesis about the mission of the church universal. There are many church documents and resources on this, so they need not be rehashed here. What is important is that the dialogue between the pastor and his parish, especially its leadership, begins with the mission of the church universal, moves to the mission of the diocese, and then addresses the mission of the parish. That order is important so that the participants approach planning with a perspective that is larger than just their own parish. Adult catechesis based in deep dialogue, education, and formation about mission in this order often makes the matter of a mission statement a very simple matter. Taking time to catechize and dialogue about the mission at the level of universal church is well worth the effort. The purpose of the catechetical formation and dialogue about mission in the different levels of the church is to bring the parish to a deeper understanding, appreciation, and experience of *communio*. At its best this part of the planning process should be experienced as a shared conversation to Christ and his redemptive purpose. A common understanding of the mission of the parish and this context makes planning both easier and more formative of the community in itself. As an unnamed bishop once said to his planner: "It is more important that people share an understanding of the mission than that they have a mission statement to nail on the wall."

Data-informed planning means that planning is based in reality. Good parish planning requires a shared understanding of the current reality in which the parish finds itself. There is the story of the parish council that described the parish to its new pastor as a blue-collar, middle-class parish of families whose membership went back many generations. The new pastor drove down the street and saw signs over stores in multiple languages, and at Mass the following Sunday he looked out to a community gathered for Eucharist that represented many races and languages. The picture given by the parish council was not wrong, just incomplete. What the council offered as fact was actually a preference to have the parish remain as it always was. That new pastor asked at the next parish council meeting what was changing in the local community, and they began to tell the pastor in great detail how the area had changed, and that the parish membership had changed. The new pastor then asked the planning office of his diocese for help with some demographic analysis and began asking his parish council to look at the data, discuss what it meant for the future of the parish, and tell stories of "the way things used to be." The best planning includes both data *and* story. Both are necessary for understanding the current reality of a parish.

Over three hundred years ago, St. Ignatius of Loyola articulated discernment as a process that is for anyone who genuinely seeks the will of God. There are plenty of resources available on the discernment process. A great book to help educate parish leadership on the use of spiritual discernment is *Discerning the Will of God: An Ignatian Guide to Christian Decision Making* by Timothy Gallagher.[1] The emphasis for planning purposes here is on the necessity of coming to planning with an open mind and singularity of purpose: the mission of the church. It means setting aside personal agendas and preferences in the same way that, when we pray, we say "your will not mine be done." Approaching planning as a discernment process means that the parish is seeking the will of God. This is very different from any corporate or civic planning process that seeks the efficient path to profit or that reflects the "will of the people." Different purposes lead to different processes. It means that while it is good to gather people who cover a wide cross section of the community, they are not representatives in the "civic representation" sense. A parish council is not a city council, a public school board, any other civic body, or a corporate board. Those who gather to do parish planning have only one purpose: to further the mission of the church. People experience stronger *communio* when they are focused on the mission of the church, prayerfully discern the will of God, and embrace gifts within the parish. Unlike other experiences of planning that parishioners may have, planning meetings are prayerful, reflective, and even contemplative at times, as well as occasions for lively interaction.

It is common for parish planning groups to say that they use a consensus model for decision-making. This is just fine as long as there is a common understanding of what "consensus" means in a Catholic context. In civic realms it often refers to a group coming to agreement. In our Catholic context it refers to everyone knowing what options are viable and potentially represent the will of God (rather than everyone agreeing on the one recommendation offered to the pastor). In this framework for consensus, political activity is less likely and the open-mindedness required for discerning the will of God—as described by Ignatius—is made possible. Self-will and imposing self-will on others cannot be the center of consensus in the Catholic Church. This implies that members of planning groups are mature enough to move beyond self-will into a focus on mission and have the capacity to keep that mission in mind as they discern practical conclusions for the parish with their pastor.

Who Leads Planning?

The *munera* of the pastor includes governance of the parish. This makes the pastor the leader of parish planning. He does not, however, do that alone. It is common for the parish council to lead the planning process with their pastor. It is also common to engage a special planning task force whose mandate from the pastor is to lead the process. Furthermore, it is common for such a group, usually composed of between seven to twelve members, to report to him through the parish council.

Gathering the right people to lead the process is perhaps the most important decision to make as planning begins. It is crucial to have around the planning table people who are capable of fully participating in *communio* at this time in their lives and who are not carrying a particularly divisive agenda or cause into the process. There are specific competency sets that may be useful: some may be facilitators of open parish meetings, some may help with data collection or data analysis, and some may be creative in developing options. All need to be spiritually mature enough to enter the discernment process with an open heart.

It sometimes happens that a pastor comes to a parish and finds the leadership of the parish underdeveloped and not ready to help him lead planning. In this case it is often very helpful to undertake some leadership development with his key people: members of the parish and finance councils, lead staff, and himself. One great program can be found described on the website of the National Leadership Roundtable on Church Management under the tab for the *Catholic Leadership 360* program.[2] It meets the criteria for developing Catholic leaders in that it is designed specifically for both the ordained and laity, it offers a well-researched and long-term impact, it is not time-intensive (your best leaders are usually the busiest people), it is relatively inexpensive, and it is clearly Catholic. This leadership development could be considered a worthwhile "pre-planning" investment.

The Steps of Parish Planning

The canonist Robert Kennedy outlined five steps in an ecclesial decision-making process whenever there are significant decisions to be made.[3] They may seem complex at first glance, but in practice they are relatively simple. Kennedy's five steps are:

1. Competent gathering and analyzing the right information
2. Developing and weighing options
3. Asking decision makers to prayerfully consider and choose among the options
4. Implementation of decisions
5. Refining the decisions

These five steps provide a solid basis for a series of steps to guide a process of parish planning along the lines of the adaptive model described above.[4]

1. Clarity of mission and boundaries. This is an opportunity for the pastor, perhaps along with an outside resource, to teach his people. What is important is that those directly involved in the planning process, as well as the parish as a whole, have the opportunity to come to a deeper and shared understanding of the mission of the church universal, the diocese, and the parish.

Parish planning operates within some boundaries, usually best set by the pastor before it begins. Some boundaries may come from the teachings of the church, while others may be financial. For example:

- the plan must keep within a balanced budget
- the plan must be consistent with what the bishop has in mind for local parishes
- the plan must include outreach to people not currently served by the parish but who live within its borders

It is also common for a pastor to set boundaries regarding how long the planning process may take.

A common way of setting boundaries is to set out three columns, listing the acceptable means for fulfilling the mission, any unacceptable means, and reasons for why such planning is necessary. Creating consensus on the boundaries of parish planning sets the rules, so to speak, before the process gets into full swing. This necessary step will make a big difference in later planning discussions.

2. Scan the current reality. A simple beginning to this can be to ask groups of parishioners to name what is changing in and around the parish in terms of three questions:

- What is emerging now?
- What is peaking right now?
- What is declining or has disappeared from view in recent years?

A subcommittee that focuses on key trends and influences can collect data by:

- Accessing demographic trends within the current parish community and the community within which the parish exists
- Surveying the needs of parish members
- Identifying parish financial, giving, and membership trends

Some other good questions for an analytics subcommittee to address include:

- Who is or is not being served (regardless of intention)?
- What do you regard as the gold standards of high quality or best practice in parish ministry?

- What influences access to high-quality ministry in the parish?
- What would need to leave or be let go of for the good of the parish's mission?
- What stories are told within the parish that tell us who we are, and to what degree are they still true?

Not all data is useful. In fact, too much data can be confusing. An important part of good planning is limiting the data to only what is useful. This step can engage many parishioners through their input. Collecting, assembling, synthesizing, and analyzing data can be a good use of the gifts of parishioners, many of whom may not be on a committee, but would be willing to serve on a special "analytics subcommittee" that does its job with the data and then ceases to exist. Trends are more important than data-points, especially for parish membership, participation in parish liturgies and ministries, and financial performance. Sometimes, especially when a parish is looking at significant demographic or economic changes, professional help with data is needed and may be available from the diocese or consultants. Check with the diocese first because, among other things, they are usually cheaper than external consultants! Some of the best information for planning is an assessment of the current ministries and management. A great tool for this is one based on the "balanced scorecard" model.[5]

One of the basic principles of collecting and analyzing data is that those who participate in its collection need the analysis fed back to them so that they know they were heard and their efforts were useful. When a valid analysis is available, a synthesis of the analysis is often provided to the parish in writing at a meeting to which all are invited. This helps the parish-at-large gain ownership of the process. This is also where the next step begins.

3. Develop a shared understanding of the current reality of the parish. This consists of the planning group reducing the amount of information collected and analyzed to seven to twelve key descriptors and putting it into a format that is easy to communicate to the parish community. One useful way of thinking about this is to imagine a car dashboard and its gauges that give limited but valuable information. Often information prepared for the parish at this point is in the form of just a couple of pages of graphics and bullet points. Further details may be made available upon request. Many parishes distribute this material at a parish meeting led by those who created it, and ask for feedback as to whether it accurately reflects people's experience, surprises anyone, or what particularly grabs one's attention. It is also common to ask if the material changes the image people have of the parish, particularly when a parish has seen significant demographic change. This may lead to further review and changes to the material used by the planning group. What is important is that there is a shared understanding that the information presented is an accurate picture of the current reality.[6]

4. Develop and evaluate viable options for parish priorities over the next two to three years. This is the creative and (dare it be said) fun part of planning. It is where the planning group and the pastor develop a list of potential priorities for the next two to three years, keeping in mind the reality in which the parish finds itself. Many priorities are created, but few can be chosen. All those that are viable must fit the current reality of the parish, including the financial situation. The potential short list of priorities is then taken to the parish community (sometimes in a series of gatherings) for comment about the strengths, weaknesses, opportunities, and challenges within each of the proposed priorities. Sometimes new options for priorities emerge. Some parishes repeat this evaluative process with the parish to make sure that all who want to get engaged and own the outcome.

5. Choose three to seven priorities for the next two to three years. Based on parish feedback the pastor, in consultation with his leadership, prayerfully considers the options and finalizes the priorities for the next two to three years.

6. Create key steps and benchmarks for progress for the next two to three years. This is where the planning group, often with staff assistance, examines the priorities and makes a list under each one of the major means for making them happen (often called "strategies") and benchmarks for progress over the next two to three years, adding a timeframe for achieving getting those benchmarks. In this way the pastor and parish council can measure progress in the plan.

7. Assess resources. The strategies of the plan need resources. This may include human resources, finances, and facilities. The parish finance council is consulted at this time. If the plan is already aligned with current reality, the basic financial and other resource considerations are most likely already in place. However, sometimes a plan may need to be changed because of resources at this point. This may mean, for example, that a priority or a strategy may need to rest "in the parking lot" for a time (not forgotten—it was important enough to be chosen so it should not be forgotten) until resources can be found for that priority or strategy. A parish budget is basically the pastoral plan of the parish aligned with the resources of the parish. The budget should always be closely aligned with the plan.

8. *Implement the plan.* Itemizing this step may seem superfluous to those not familiar with the planning process, but part of planning is to see that the plan is actually implemented. A plan is not done until it is acted upon. Otherwise, of what use is the plan? This means attaching a "who is taking responsibility for what by when" level of detail—at least to the initial steps of the plan and ensuring that those first steps are in motion. This is where many parish plans fail.[7]

It is also true that the best plan will not be implemented if the context of the plan is poor parish management. The most effective tool for moving toward great management in parishes is the *Catholic Standards for Excellence*, a well-researched and easily adopted set of management standards for Catholic parishes (see the previous chapter by Michael Brough).[8]

9. *Evaluation.* No plan is perfect, and so there is a need for ongoing refinement. This is often done with staff and the parish council in a monitoring role on behalf of and reporting regularly to the pastor. A monthly review by the parish council of "who has done what" is often useful.

Integrating Planning into the Life of the Parish

Planning in the adaptive mode does not occur as an isolated event. It is part of what the pastor and his leadership groups integrate into their annual agenda cycle. The initial planning process is described above. On an annual basis the parish council engages in a scanning process asking the appropriate questions to determine if the conditions under which the parish is operating have changed significantly enough to warrant adapting the plan to the new circumstances. This is the "adaptive" of adaptive planning. Perhaps a new priority is warranted. Perhaps a particular strategy is not working for one of the priorities. Perhaps there has been a sudden decline or rise in membership, and so the pastor and parish lay leadership ask themselves why this has happened and how this impacts the plan. Perhaps the cultural diversity of the parish has changed and attention needs to be given to that in liturgies. The need for a major planning process is minimized by the ongoing adaptive work of the pastor and his parish leadership. There may eventually come a time when the conditions for the parish change so significantly that an entirely new planning process is warranted, but this is not common if the adaptive work has been ongoing.

How a parish integrates adaptive planning into the life of the parish leadership is described as a seven-meeting cycle spread throughout the year:

- Scan the current reality (1 meeting)
- Develop options for changing priorities and/or strategies for adaptation to new operating conditions and weigh those options (2 meetings)
- Relate the choices that the leadership makes to the budget (1 meeting in close consultation with the parish finance council)
- Adopt the newly adapted plan and its budget (2 meetings)
- Evaluate the mission effectiveness of implementing the plan (1 meeting)

At every parish council meeting time should be set aside for discussing progress toward the plan's benchmarks and how to keep the parish moving forward in its priorities. Embedding this process into the life of the parish council ensures that the plan remains relevant and implementation is having an impact on the mission focus of the parish.[9]

Documenting a Parish Plan

We began by saying that a parish plan is a set of relationships based on certain well-defined agreements. Remember that the plan is not the document itself but the shared understandings and agreements within the living relationships that make up the parish. It is also important, however, to document the plan so that it may outlive its creators and be shared and received within the larger context of *communio*. It becomes a reference guide for the parish council through which they measure progress and a resource to focus staff on the mission and to orient new staff. It is used whenever major decisions—financial or otherwise—are made.

When documenting a parish plan the adage "less is more" applies. The first three elements of the plan that form the basis for the relationship we call a plan are Mission, Vision, and Priorities. These may all be documented on one sheet of paper. Each of the three to four priorities should then have its own column on the following page, where the strategies for implementing each priority and dated benchmarks for progress (spaced about every three to six months) are listed. The names of those accountable for each strategy and benchmark are also listed. This makes a valuable reference document for the pastor, parish council, and staff and is small enough to be easily distributed to the parish. The key descriptions of the reality that informed the development of the plan are also documented as a one- or two-page synthesis. Again, such brevity makes it easy to distribute to the community. Some communities also prefer to have a detailed version available as well. Experience shows, however, that a highly detailed plan has limited value and that a document of no more than two or three pages is much more pragmatic.

The Role of the Pastor in Planning

While every pastor is different and has his own preferences for defining his role, there are some common roles that the most successful pastors take in parish planning.

First, the most successful pastors stay faithful to their *munera* by remaining in governance rather than management. In other words, don't abdicate the important role of oversight by spending all your time managing the details. Leave that to the gifted volunteers and staff who want to help you succeed. For example, teach and catechize the faithful on the mission of the universal church and set the boundaries of the process, but then let those who have process management training and expertise do what they are good at. Leverage the strengths around you rather than trying to do it all yourself.

Second, avoid the trap of using a corporate or civic model for planning. Stick to a model that is derived from Catholic teaching and tradition and that plays to your training and strength. In other words, use a model based in prayer and discernment that engages the lay leaders and the parishioners in reading the signs of the times (as the church has done for hundreds of years). Prayerfully discern with the help of the laity (as again the church has always done) the will of God for how to respond in this time and place to the current reality in which the church must fulfill her mission.

Third, be the decision-maker as is your proper role as pastor, but only after you have heard the prayerful and contemplative reflections of the parish leadership. Listen to what God is telling you through their voices with all the humility of one whom God has called to be his servant. Do this and the parish community under your leadership will be doing God's will in a planned and coherent way. And you will be a most effective shepherd of God's people.

A Final Word

Finally, there are two things every pastor who is engaged in pastoral planning should keep in mind. The first is the favorite prayer of almost every pastoral planner I have known: *God grant me the serenity to accept the things that cannot be changed, courage to change the things which should be changed, and the wisdom to distinguish the one from the other.* The second is the words of Jesus himself from scripture: *Not my will, but yours be done.*

Endnotes

1. Timothy Gallagher, *Discerning the Will of God: An Ignatian Guide to Christian Decision Making* (New York: Crossroads, 2009).

2. See *Catholic Leadership 360* (National Leadership Roundtable on Church Management, 2013), www.theleadershiproundtable.org.

3. See Robert Kennedy, "Shared Responsibility in Ecclesial Decision-Making," *Studia Canonica* 14 (1980): 5-23.

4. Dennis Cheesebrow and Jim Lundholm-Eades, "Five Steps for Parish Planning" (working paper, Leadership Roundtable on Church Management, 2005).

5. See National Leadership Roundtable on Church Management, *An Assessment Tool for Parish Leadership Relationships, Parish Ministry and Management* (2008), www.theleadershiproundtable.org/churchepedia/docs/NLRCMLeader shipRelationshipAssessmentToolv708082008.pdf.

6. Some great insights for this part of the planning process may be found in Dennis Cheesebrow, *Partnership Redefined: Leadership Through the Power of &*. (Centerville, MN: Bogman Publishing, 2012). His framework's diagrams and their explanations deserve particular attention.

7. There are some valuable insights from corporate business literature on implementing a plan. Two of the best that are worth asking parish leadership— certainly a parish council and finance council, as well as ministry staff—to read and discuss are Gino Wickman, *Traction: Get a Grip on Your Business* (Dallas: Benbella Books, 2011) and Larry Bossidy, Ram Charan, and Charles Burck, *Execution: The Discipline of Getting Things Done* (Dallas: Benbella Books, 2002).

8. See National Leadership Roundtable on Church Management *Catholic Standards for Excellence* (2013). Available at www.theleadershiproundtable .org. Also helpful for pastors and parish staff members is Barry Oshrey, *In the Middle* (Boston: Power and Systems, 1994).

9. I have described this kind of cycle in Jim Lundholm-Eades, "The Parish Pastoral Council: *Communio* in Action," www.theleadershiproundtable.org /churchepedia/docs/ParishPastoralCouncils.doc.

Unity in Diversity

Arturo Chávez

The increasingly multicultural composition of our churches is a modern-day reality, and the implications for the pastoral or priestly ministry are huge. Actually, diversity has been a part of the Catholic Church since its origins. And now, two thousand years later, we can see that sometimes we responded correctly, sometimes we didn't. This presents many challenges as well as many opportunities to you as pastors.

Chances are you're already living with priests, or in a community of priests, from other countries. And this great coming together has implications on multiple levels—in our ministry, in our work, and in our daily lives. The truth is, we all need development and ongoing formation as ministers.

It seems like everyone today is talking about culture, and everyone is trying to get up to speed about what it means for the future. One sector that's been paying close attention to culture for decades and is quite serious about its challenges and opportunities—particularly from a marketing standpoint—is business. And so I intend to draw from the wisdom of that sector in this presentation.

Here in the United States, our church and our bishops are calling on us to pay attention to culture but not primarily as an academic exercise. That's not to say the church doesn't encourage academic rigor when it comes to preparing for the ministry in a different cultural setting. But an academic study of culture is not sufficient for the call of the Gospel to proclaim the Good News of Jesus to every nation. Rather, the bishops and our church for the past two centuries have been calling on us to see the connection and the interplay of culture and faith. And so, just as

138

grace builds on nature, we come to know the Gospel, we come to hear the Good News, in a particular language that is rooted in a particular culture. That's where God comes to us in who we are and loves us for who we are and how we are in the world. God doesn't discriminate among cultures; in God's eyes, there is no perfect culture.

According to this definition, culture is a gift that's handed down by our ancestors from generation to generation. So often, however, especially in the work that you do as priests and pastors, culture emerges as a challenge, as a "problem." How are we going to deal with this? How are we going to solve this problem of diversity, instead of working from the premise that culture is a gift?

There are many people, like my great-grandmother, who came from Europe and moved to Mexico when land was being given to settlers to expand the frontiers. And so these people mixed with those already on the land, making Latinos a mixture of cultures.

I mention this to you because we're not really born *with* a culture. We're born *into* a culture. That culture is given to us. In a very real way, it is our interior landscape, the landscape of our soul. So much of culture is adapting to an environment, adapting to a place and time. And I can assure you, that process works. It continues to be handed down from one generation to the next.

At the same time, though, culture is dynamic. In other words, being Mexican, or Mexican American, is very different for me than it was for my mother or my great-grandmother. And it's different for my two daughters now, one who is sixteen and the other fourteen.

So, culture is the core of our identity. Just like with our psychological development and identity formation, it happens in our very early years and becomes an integral part of us. And though we can change many parts of our identity, there are other parts that remain constant throughout our lives. Culture is one of these. It influences everything we do and how we relate to the world. Yet it's such an intrinsic part of us that we're not even aware of it. It's like the air that we breathe.

Cultural Friction

Sadly, the way we usually get to know other people's cultures is by bumping into them, by seeing them all in the same pew on Sunday morning, for example. And these encounters sometimes take the form of cultural clashes, instead of cultural celebrations. We don't have the chance to learn about the other person's beliefs and values in areas like the meaning of beauty and cleanliness, and their sense of space and order.

To give you an example of the latter, at the Mexican American Catholic College, all of our bedrooms have two nice beds. And all guests have the option of either double or single occupancy. Inevitably, most people from cultures that are not Latino take the single occupancy—they want their space, even if it's just for one night—while those of us from a Latino background, especially laypeople, often want double occupancy. We want to have a roommate, someone with whom we can talk and share our experiences.

The important message here is that most of the time one culturally specific way isn't better than the other. Both have strengths, both have limitations. Once again, culture is our inner clock; it was activated by our ancestors. You may come from a culture where wasting time is frowned upon. Time is money and it must be treated as such. And so, your understanding of time is very exact. It tends to be very forward-looking. On the other hand, there are many cultures where the measurement of time is much more cyclical. It's more grounded in experiences and relationships—both past and present—than it is on money and the future.

There are situations, of course, where these different cultural orientations come into conflict. It could happen within your parish council. Let's say I've scheduled a council meeting for 7 p.m. I expect people to be there on time, so I can end the meeting on time. And most council members are compliant. Except for a couple—who come from a culture where time is primarily about relationships and not money. It is a much more relaxed sense of time and they show up at 7:40, well after the meeting has started. They come in smiling, offer me a warm greeting, greet others with a hug, and take their seat. What's my reaction? Well, I'm seething inside. At the same time, though, I know that not returning the greeting would be interpreted as extremely rude in this person's culture, especially if they're elderly and especially if they pass in front of me. Indeed, the reason they're here is because *I'm* here—because I asked them to come. So I swallow my anger and do the culturally correct thing: I smile back and welcome them to the meeting.

Communicating through Culture

As you can see, these kinds of cultural protocols are often expressed in how we communicate—either with or without words. So, the expressions we grow up with become little truths within us. Let me explain what I mean.

Straddling cultures as I do—including Mexican, American, and youth culture—I started an organization in San Antonio to help get kids, mostly those in gangs, off the streets. Part of our program was designed to bring together people of different cultures in a spirit of unity and friendship. We learned a lot about ourselves, and we learned a lot about each other. One day, we were having a staff meeting, and we started talking about a problem that had arisen. In the midst of the discussion, I said, "You know what? We have to nip this problem in the butt." Well, the Mexicanos at the table were in full agreement, nodding their heads, while the white staff members—there were only a couple of them—looked perplexed. One of them, with whom I had become good friends, came up to me after the meeting and said, "Arturo, I think what you meant to say in the meeting was 'nip it in the bud,' with a *d*."

That's where the cultural distinction comes into play. Remember, I grew up in a rough neighborhood where most people keep dogs for protection. So, "nip it in the butt" made perfect sense to me and my friends, whereas "nip it in the bud" made no sense in a culture like ours that loves flowers. So again, culture impacts how we communicate and how we interpret idioms and sayings.

Similarly, the tone and volume we take in communicating has differing cultural meanings. You might go to a parishioner's home for dinner and be taken aback by family members talking to each other really loudly and brusquely gesturing back and forth. They seem to be arguing with one another, and you begin to wonder where all this anger comes from. It isn't until you run into the parishioner a week later and express your consternation that he tells you there's no anger at all within the family. "That's just the way we talk, Father," he says. "Don't take it too seriously." On the other hand, you might be invited to a dinner with another family where no one says a word; they're just not communicating. And thinking like a pastor, you wonder how you're going to get this family to reconcile. As it turns out, they get along just fine. They just don't talk much during dinner. In their culture, silence means something completely different.

This brings me back to where we started: the nexus of culture and religion. How we feel about God—when and where and how often we relate to God. Each of these is linked to our culture, to how we relate culturally to the divine. In some cultures, our religion and our faith are so important that we feel we have to tell everyone about them. We have to make others become one of us by knocking on their doors, handing out pamphlets, and converting them to our religion. In other cultures, religion and faith are so sacred, so special, that no one else is allowed in. You have to be born into it.

In the world of business, Edward T. Hall has been influential in many cross-cultural studies.[1] He's fond of comparing culture to an iceberg. We're all familiar with the saying, "That's only the tip of the iceberg," connoting the fact that the greatest part of the mass lies beneath the surface of the water, invisible to people. And so it is with culture, according to Hall. There's the part that we can see, taste and feel, the part that we're taught, like how to do a particular dance, how to celebrate a birthday, or how to introduce ourselves to people using the names of our ancestors.

But the vast part of culture is invisible, the underwater realm of values, attitudes, mind-sets, and spirituality. Especially with spirituality, we get into the realm of the internal, the unconscious, the implicitly learned. Someone may ask you, "Where did you learn that?" and you respond, "I don't know." In truth, there is no answer. That's just what it means to be Mexican, or German, or French, or whatever your culture happens to be.

That's all well and good. But what happens when your culture rubs up against mine and two people from totally different cultures come face-to-face? According to Hall, this is the definition of a cultural clash, and it occurs not in the external part of the iceberg but in the murky, underwater realm.

Here's how the friction can occur. As a pastor, I may outwardly think that I love this group of new parishioners; they're so joyful, so friendly, but inwardly, I'm annoyed because they don't come to Mass on time. Or outwardly, I may appreciate a husband and wife in our parish because they're so professional, so organized, but inwardly I distrust them because they appear so cold, never shaking my hand or looking me in the eye.

Building Unity from Diversity

Where do these feelings come from? I know I'm a good person and that I don't want to feel this way or be a hypocrite. What the church and the U.S. bishops tell us is, these cultural confrontations—or cultural clashes, as Hall would call them—are very valuable and opportune moments in our lives. For it's through these often painful interactions that we have an opportunity for conversion where, if we're attentive, we encounter Jesus Christ and have the opportunity to build unity from diversity, not in spite of it.

In his apostolic exhortation to the Church in America, Pope John Paul II called us to an encounter with the living Jesus Christ.[2] This encounter sets up a process which brings us to a greater conversion, which leads us to a deeper communion, which leads us to a global solidarity or unity beyond geographic and cultural borders. The catch is, you can't get to the unity part without first experiencing the conversion.

People tend to think of conversion as a dramatic turnabout: the blind man who is now able to see, or the criminal who becomes a model citizen. For most of us, however, conversion is another way of expressing ongoing growth. Usually, true growth involves some pain, some vulnerability, some letting go. It often means suspending my agenda, suspending my judgments.

The bishops have raised some fundamental questions here. First, can our hearts be open to others, particularly to those who are very different from us? And, in our encounter with others, will we be open to the experience of conversion and, just as importantly, to the processes of change and growth? As the saying goes, change is inevitable, but growth is optional. And that's the option we're called on to make—the option for ongoing conversion.

How Does Conversion Occur?

We know that it's a process and that it usually begins with a state that anthropology labels "ethnocentrism." Ethnocentrism is basically the assumption that everyone sees the world as I do. It's like a room filled with mirrors, in which I see only myself. If you're like most people, you tend to surround yourself with others who are like you. This is especially true in our early years. You see evidence of it everywhere: in schools, for example, or even in the parish when you're having a dinner and the Mexicans, the Blacks, and the Filipinos sit in their respective groups. It's only natural that we gravitate toward people who are like us. That's how we begin life. We don't know any other way.

The Stages of Cultural Development

But how do we get beyond ethnocentrism? Sociologist Milton Bennett has identified various stages, which he refers to as the development of intercultural sensitivity.[3]

The first stage is denial that differences even exist. Perhaps we haven't been outside our neighborhood, and therefore we haven't been exposed to other nationalities and ways of life. So, denial is the belief that differences simply don't exist. And if they do exist, they're something that must be changed or suppressed. At the Mexican American Catholic College, for instance, we get many calls from priests—usually prompted by bishops—asking if we have an accent eradication program for new priests from foreign countries. We never call it accent eradication, however, even if the literature does. We refer to it as "mastering U.S. pronunciation of English."

The next major stage of cultural development is what Bennett identifies as the defense stage. He sums it up this way: if you're different, you're bad. Here's an example. Let's say you have an international food night at your parish, where everyone brings a dish from his/her country. You walk around to the various tables, and someone asks you to sample his/her specialty. You take a look at the dish, and your stomach turns inside out. So you say very politely, "No, thank you. I'm really not hungry."

What you're really saying is, "I don't like your food, so I'll take a pass." When you think about it, we often take the same close-minded approach to people who behave differently from us. We may not be conscious of it, but we do it anyway. We're on autopilot. We take the attitude that if people come to America, they should become Americans (whatever that means), and do what Americans do. They should leave behind their culture and their language. We are not open to "the other."

An outgrowth of this negative attitude is the notion that culture and cultural differences are problems or challenges that divert us from more important matters. For example, we may have a request from a small group of parishioners to conduct a Mass in Korean and think to ourselves: they have to be kidding. How would we ever pull off that one? Or we may grumble about another group of church members who want us to translate into Spanish our guidelines on who can receive Communion. This isn't why I became a priest, you tell yourself. You're already overwhelmed with your ministry, and now you're expected to take on the added burden of cultural diversity.

Another unfortunate consequence of the defense stage is the belief by members of diverse or minority cultures—particularly children—that because they're different, they *are* bad. And that other people are good. They begin to think if they leave their language behind, if they change their name from Arturo to Arthur, or Ricardo to Richard—if they essentially forsake their culture—perhaps they'll be accepted.

Next we enter the stage of cultural development which Bennett calls minimization. It's moving beyond the denial and the defense stages and coming to an understanding and an appreciation that others *do* have distinct cultures. And it's attempting to get a handle on these cultures by identifying what's in the iceberg under the water—what are their values, for example, and how do they look upon the concept of time. Above all, minimization means getting beyond the stereotypes and the differences that can create conflicts between cultures.

As I travel around the country, people come up to me from time to time and say, "You're Mexican? I thought all Mexicans were short." I'm not offended by it anymore, because to me it's a positive thing, an acknowledgment that they're moving beyond the stereotype of what a Mexican looks like.

As Catholics, our goal is unity and oneness, the knowledge that we are all brothers and sisters in Christ. A helpful image for me is a simple room. Instead of being filled with mirrors, where we see the world only one way—in our image—this room is filled with doors. If we step outside, there are many directions in which to go, many different ways to see the world. And yet—here is the important part—we always have the ability to return to our room. That's the cultural piece that continues to live within us, even as we change, even as we adapt to other cultures.

So, through minimization, we begin to make adjustments, to accept differences in both values and behavior of other people, and resolve that we are not going to rush to judge other people. Just because someone hasn't said a word at a meeting or sits with a stern face in the back of the church during our homily doesn't mean he/she is angry or bored. In that culture, it may simply be a way of giving us undivided attention.

The Last Stage: Cultural Integration

Finally, we begin to adapt and integrate. We have ventured out so often through the doors I mentioned before, that we see things differently now. We've reached the point where we can integrate these differences into our own identities. Missionaries typically experience this phenomenon. And at this point, something new and wonderful is created within the parish that has its roots not entirely from my culture and not entirely from theirs. It's created because people are willing to go beyond their normal comfort zones. This cultural integration is what the Catholic Church calls us to. It's the ultimate goal of conversion—a way of affirming our continuous growth while suspending our private agendas and judgments.

Integration is also a way of learning to do contextual evaluation. What do I mean by that? Contextual evaluation is knowing that not all values in life are fixed. Our faith tells us that abortion, rape, torture are intrinsic evils that are wrong in any culture. There are no gray areas here. But as pastors, we know that other values are not always cloaked in such absolutes; they sometimes wear shades of gray. How do we make this determination while holding firm to those beliefs where there can be no compromise? Contextual evaluation provides a platform to make this possible. We can firmly hold to the truth, even as we seek to build a common ground by trying to see the world through the eyes of the other—understanding his values and why they are so important. This does not mean that I have to change my beliefs; rather, I am so conscious and firm in my own that I am not threatened by differences and I can prayerfully discern between what is essential and what can be adapted without compromising my core belief system.

I keep coming back to this notion of conversion as the great cultural equalizer. Conversion, however, is uncomfortable. It's painful. It moves us beyond our comfort zone, which is why we would rather not do it. If I come from a culture with a history of enslavement or violence, part of my challenge of moving outside my comfort zone might be to speak up, to embrace the fact that Jesus empowers all of us for ministry. "You will receive power," he proclaims.

And there is certainly no better or more satisfying example of the power we confer than the ability to bring about intercultural sensitivity among the members of our parish by showing them the way. We indeed have the ability to foster cultural integration by opening our hearts to others, particularly to those who are different from us, and rising above the differences and stereotypes. And in the course of these encounters, we become one with Jesus Christ, opening ourselves to the life-affirming processes of change and personal growth and, most important, to the transformative power of conversion.

Endnotes

1. See Edward T. Hall, *The Hidden Dimension* (New York: Anchor Books, 1966).

2. John Paul II, Post-Synodal Apostolic Exhortation, *Ecclesia in America* (22 January 1999).

3. See, e.g., Janet M. Bennett and Milton J. Bennett, "Developing Intercultural Sensitivity: An Integrative Approach to Global and Domestic Diversity," in *Handbook of Intercultural Training*, third ed., edited by Dan Landis, Janet M. Bennett, and Milton J. Bennett (Thousand Oaks, CA: SAGE Publications, 2004), 147–65.

14

The Pastor and the Diocese

Franklyn Casale

I would like to begin with a personal reflection. I was a very happy parish priest, ordained seven years, when all of a sudden I was swooped up and put down in the chancery office of the Newark Archdiocese. Never in a million years could I have envisioned myself being part of the chancery office, as it was called in those days. But it proved to be a valuable learning experience for me. The first thing I had to do, though, was make myself realize I wasn't giving up the ministry. I was simply doing it now in a different way; I was still making a contribution to the church.

Indeed, I had a very fulfilling experience as a curate in those days. I became secretary to the archbishop. And after two years of knowing very little, I finally learned the job, and about the archbishop. Having just celebrated his seventieth anniversary of priesthood and still doing confirmations at the age of ninety-seven, Archbishop Peter Gerety [who has now celebrated his one-hundredth birthday] is a wonderful man, a great teacher, and an excellent communicator. I learned a tremendous amount from him, and when he retired, I felt like he had conferred on me another degree. He was that good a teacher.

I'm telling you this story because I liked to consider myself ministering to the priests when I worked in the Office of the Archdiocese. And I think that most of the people in those offices today look at what they're doing in the same way. They see themselves as helping you to be successful. St. Thomas University in Florida, where I now serve as president, is owned by the Archdiocese of Miami, so I still interface with the Pastoral Center, as it's now called. And I can tell you that the people who work in these offices—especially laypeople—have enormous regard for the priests. I think it's important for you to realize that so you don't hesitate to interact with them. They really see themselves as doing ministry, not just business, and I encourage you to take advantage of this very valuable resource at the diocesan level.

The other thing I can tell you about the people in the diocesan office is, they're going to know a lot more about you than you'd ever think. In fact, they're going to know almost everything about you and your parish. They'll get to know your administrative style. And what inevitably happens is, there's about 10 percent of us guys who they have to "pick up after," so to speak. My strong advice to you is this: don't become one of those 10 percent. Whatever you do in your parish, be among the 90 percent that do it right—not the ones that the Pastoral Center, or chancery, is constantly picking up after.

The Evolution of the Parish

With that as backdrop, I'd like to very briefly cover the historical development of parishes. I'm sure you already know much of this, but I think it's important to review it in light of your new role as pastors.

In the early church, the bishops were the pastors. And for almost four centuries, because of persecutions and the fact the church was not yet recognized, there was just a very loose organization of bishops. When Constantine proclaimed religious toleration throughout the Roman Empire in 313, the church became public, and the bishops ordained and sent forth priests into various regions to minister to the people as part of a spreading faith. Up to the eleventh century, the structure of the parish was influenced by the medieval feudal system and was dependent on the support of local lords. As part of the Gregorian Reform, Gregory VII reconstituted the parish and made it more dependent on the local bishop. The parochial structure he instituted remained substantially unchanged until the twentieth century.

With the Second Vatican Council, the parish structure changed again, from juridical to communal, or "communion." So, we enter as pastors into a pastoral communion, and I'd like to cover with you some of its components. Even in the early church, all the disciples were in communion with one another. And today, of course, we share communion with the bishop. We also share communion with the whole presbyterium through our ordination by the bishop. *Christus Dominus*, the decree of the Second Vatican Council concerning the pastoral office of bishops, talks about the fact that priests share with the bishop the biblical office of shepherding.[1] And under canon law—which as you know, was revised after the Second Vatican Council—the pastor should assure that the parish community recognizes its membership in the diocese and the universal church.

The reason I emphasize this is because you need to see yourselves as pastors in communion with the bishop, whether you like him or not. The fact is, you share his priesthood. And it's not necessarily your parish. It's the people's parish.

I remember a venerable priest of the Archdiocese of Newark saying to me, "It's so great when you get your feet under your own table. But, that's about all you own in the parish—your own table. The rest belongs to the people or the diocese." And we're shepherding the people on behalf of the bishop in the diocese.

The role of the bishop is underscored by the Catechism in its definition of a parish.[2] I found this description rich and dynamic and realized it would be helpful to review it. It reads:

> "A *parish* is a definite community of the Christian faithful established on a stable basis within a particular church; the pastoral care of the parish is entrusted to a pastor as its own shepherd under the authority of the diocesan bishop." (*Code of Canon Law*, c. 515§1.) It is the place where all the faithful can be gathered together for the Sunday celebration of the Eucharist. The parish initiates the Christian people into the ordinary expression of the liturgical life: it gathers them together in this celebration; it teaches Christ's saving doctrine; it practices the charity of the Lord in good works and brotherly love. (§2179)

Important Diocesan Resources

How does the diocese help the parish fulfill this mission? To address that, I'd like to cite some of the key diocesan resources that are available to pastors like yourselves.

First is the chief finance officer, whom you'll probably interact with more than anyone else in the diocese. You should also be able to use the services and know-how of the vicar general and moderator of the curia, who is essentially the chief operating officer of the diocese. The vicar general is always a priest, so he's going to understand your situation and needs. He is second in command of the diocese, after the bishop, and is basically in charge of the administration of the diocese. Because many of the offices report to him, he has his finger on a good deal of information that can help you, or he can point you in the right direction. Also, he can usually tip you off to what the bishop is thinking on a particular matter. The vicar general has ordinary jurisdiction, which means he can make independent decisions, though many times he won't make them without the bishop somehow getting involved. The chancellor, who can be a cleric, religious, or layperson, can assist you with policies and records. He is often the person you go to for faculties or permission for priests or for your own parishioners.

A little bit of advice, based on my experience. The chancellor and the rest of the Pastoral Center are going to pile a lot of information and chores on you, including letters, programs, activities, and the like. They'll seem to be giving you more work than you can possibly handle. What you should do is develop your priorities; pick and choose those programs which you feel will not only work best in your parish but bring some excitement and energy to it. At the same time, be respectful of your responsibility to the bishop and the diocese itself.

The judicial vicar is a key diocesan figure whose workload has grown in recent years as a result of the wide range of legal and rights issues he handles. If you need help on canonical matters, the judicial vicar is the person you want to see. His purview extends to post-marriage, while everything relating to pre-marriage, along with all dispensations, resides in the chancery part of the diocese.

Mastering Human Resources

Human resources is a big area right now. Because you've either arrived at or will soon enter a new parish, there will be people there who you think are just great and want to retain, and others you'll want to jettison. And some of them you will. But there's a wrong way and a right way to do that. You can't just go in and fire somebody because you don't like him/her. You have to be on solid ground, and there are several ways to accomplish that. One is to simply change the job description. As a matter of practice, you should write a job description for everybody who works for you. Now, let's say you have a pastoral associate and want to replace that person with a director of religious education (DRE). What you may do is change the job description, which gives you license to dismiss the pastoral associate and hire a new DRE with the requisite qualifications. You've eliminated that person by dispensing with the job.

Another way to make staff changes is by documentation. Remember, as pastor you're in charge of personnel in your parish, even if you have an administrator. And this means writing down everything—the good and the bad—about someone's job performance. Annual reviews are particularly important, even of your parochial vicars. It's good for you, and it's good for them. Truth is, we're not very good at giving credit where credit is due. And if someone is doing a commendable job, annual reviews inform the person of that. On the other hand, if they're not performing well, the most sensible way to dismiss them is to have supportive documentation. It might state, "I told this individual they needed to improve and that here are the goals that must be met. They subsequently failed to meet them." The key thing is, you need to write it all down and keep it in a file. And the diocese can be a valuable resource to you in this endeavor—in everything from job descriptions to actually taking steps to dismiss an employee.

Oftentimes, the toughest part of letting someone go is overcoming the emotional hurdle. It's very hard to dismiss someone, like a secretary or bookkeeper, who's been working in the parish for thirty years and they say to you, "You're a priest and now you're putting me out on the street?" As pastor, what you must constantly be mindful of is your fiduciary responsibility to make sure that people do their jobs. And being the parish bookkeeper for thirty years doesn't necessarily mean that person is doing the best possible job. You may need to get a professional with updated skills and training.

One of our problems is, we typically don't like to spend money on things we don't think are all that important. Well, if I can give you a bit of advice, your bookkeeper is important. And if you ask those in the chancery office—including the finance, insurance, and risk management people—they'll tell you the same thing. So, you should be willing to spend a little extra money to make sure you have somebody in that job who really knows how to keep books.

Deciphering the Financial Statement

You also need to learn how to read a financial statement. This way, when there are changes in the assets and the equity of your parish because investments decline or because you're depreciating your buildings and not making any repairs to them, you'll know and understand that from your financial statement. I urge you to sit down with a CPA or somebody who knows accounting and ask for an explanation of the financial statements. Such statements are really not that complicated, and it's to your distinct advantage to try to get your head around them.

Legal Counsel

Counsel is the next diocesan resource I'd like to discuss. Every diocese has either in-house legal counsel or hires someone to serve in that capacity as a consultant. They're available to serve the diocese as well as you and your parish. Too often, we seek out counsel only after we buy or sell property or enter into legal contracts or agreements with people and encounter problems. Well, it's much better to go to counsel and get advice before you find yourself in trouble, or in water over your head. That's why counsel is there, and I urge you to aggressively use this service. Many times you'll be fortunate enough to have some competent lawyers in your own parish, and they'll be willing to help you out. But, make sure that you communicate with the diocese and keep them fully informed of any pending legal matters.

Office of Property Management

Most of the larger dioceses have an Office of Property Management. It's not a bad idea, by the way, to sit down with someone from the chancery to find out exactly what offices are available. And don't be afraid to ask questions. If there is an Office of Property Management, it can be a tremendous help to you if you're buying or selling property. For example, they'll inspect the house you plan to buy if there is no rectory. And because it's a service the chancery offers to its parishes, there is usually no charge attached. I recommend that you, as a new pastor, invite the Office of Property Management to your site to inspect it and do a little review of your physical plant. What's the condition of the buildings, the foundations, the heating system, the air-conditioning system? It will prove very helpful for you to have this information.

The Budget

The next financial-related area I'd like to focus on is the budget. I can't overstate the importance of a good budget. Canon law, in fact, requires that you prepare and submit a financial statement each year to the diocese. Many dioceses require a budget as well for the coming year. There's a good reason for this. You need a vision of where you're going as a parish and how you're going to finance it. It must be done in a planned fashion. And because we tend to be unrealistic about what we think we can accomplish since we rarely look at the dollars and cents involved, there needs to be a sound budget and guidelines in place.

As a wonderful pastor once told me, "If you have an idea, the next thing you need is an idea of how to pay for it." On a personal note, I took over St. Thomas University in Miami at a time when the budget was operating at a three-million-dollar loss. Though some corrective action was taken even before I arrived, I said to everybody, "This is how we're going to balance our budget. We'll only spend as much as we have." And so we let people go, closed some offices, and took other steps to curb costs. And for fifteen years—up until this past year—we balanced our budget.

Insurance

As pastors, you'll have health insurance, auto insurance, property insurance, casualty insurance, liability insurance, and worker's compensation issues to deal with. As a real basic primer, casualty insurance covers you in the event someone falls on church property, for example, and is injured. Liability insurance offers you protection against being sued. For example, a teacher may strike a child in the classroom and a lawsuit is then filed by the child's parents. Worker's compensation is a state-regulated program that kicks in after a certain period of time if an employee is sick or gets injured on the job. It's important to know this because sometimes we keep paying the bills of sick or injured employees out of our pockets when worker's compensation insurance is available to absorb the costs over the long-term.

I believe almost every diocese today offers its parishes pooled insurance. As the name suggests, this arrangement spreads the risk so if a major fire occurs, your insurance premium will not go up because the risk is mitigated by all the other parishes paying premiums. So, it's really a good deal. The same principle applies to healthcare. You'll always have people telling you they can get you a better deal on healthcare insurance. But the fact is, if you have a handful of parish employees with cancer on that policy, the premiums are going to soar. If it's a pooled risk through the diocese, however, you don't have to worry. Just to repeat, the diocesan insurance pools are great resources at your fingertips.

Risk Management

Closely tied to insurance is the field of risk management. We all know there are a lot of conditions within your physical plant that are risky, things that are potential fire hazards, or things which could cause someone to trip and be injured, for example. If you're in higher education, as I am, you clearly recall the devastating fire at Seton Hall University some years ago in which lives were lost. In the wake of 9/11, Hurricane Katrina, and the tragic shootings at Virginia Tech, the federal government extended to colleges and universities what's called National Incident Management System. That system provides guidance on how all of us in higher education manage incidents and address such basic questions as who's in charge. If something unexpected happens, who makes decisions? The principal? The teacher? The fire department? The police department? You need to think this through in advance because you won't have that luxury once a major incident occurs.

Here's a hypothetical incident which illustrates the need for advance planning. Let's say children from your parish are in Vermont on a church-sponsored ski trip. Back home, the news flashes across the TV screens: "Ski lift breaks in Vermont. Fifty people critically injured." Okay. You're not there. Who's handling the incident and making decisions on-site? Have you designated someone in advance? Is there someone in the rectory besides you who can deal with parents or the press? I say other than you because at this point you don't have the time to handle parents or the press; you're trying to determine what's happening with the kids.

Perhaps they were in their hotel and weren't even close to the ski lift. And if that's the case, you still have a crisis on your hands because you have legions of frightened parents calling you, demanding to speak to their children. They can't get through to them on their cell phones because the lines are jammed.

You have to organize that in advance through an incident management plan or an emergency management plan. The government, as I mentioned, is forcing higher education to do that.

Many of you have schools. God forbid something tragic happens, like a shooter loose in the classrooms. Do you evacuate, or do you lock the classroom doors and make sure everybody stays put? Do you even have locks on your classroom doors? I would guess nobody here has a comprehensive incident plan in place. I urge you to give it serious thought. At St. Thomas University in Miami, we were fortunate enough to share a $500,000 grant with two other local universities to train our personnel and develop our emergency plans. Resources like this may also be available to you. My suggestion is to check online and reach out to your diocese for guidance and help. They can connect you with the resources you need to develop a strong emergency management plan. It's a good idea, for example, to have your police department come in, show them your floor plan, and have them organize a disaster program for you.

Banking

Regarding insurance, as mentioned above, the diocese is your best resource when it comes to banking. Even if you have a relationship with a local bank for transactions, any pool you enter into with the diocese is probably going to offer you much better returns. Indeed, many archdioceses and dioceses require that you manage your finances through them. Some have very sophisticated, paperless systems so that when you write a check, it not only hits the local bank but the chancery office as well. So, they're monitoring your finances on a regular basis.

On the subject of finances, integrity and transparency are two words that must guide your thoughts and actions each day. You must be honest and beyond reproach in every financial transaction you and your staff undertake, and you must work to ensure that every financial transaction can withstand the scrutiny of both your congregation and the public.

Remember too, there are very few things that the chancery office will not know about you and your parish.

Investments

Integrity and transparency are particularly important when it comes to investments. Here again, someone in your parish is inevitably going to approach you and say, "You know, Father, I can get you a great return on the $250,000 the parish has in the bank." First of all, thank God you have $250,000 in the bank! But what would happen if you said yes to this individual and the investment was made through a Bernie Madoff-type organization. Integrity and common sense dictate that you stick with the safest investment vehicles when it comes to the parish's money. And you can be confident that those funds will always be the safest and most fully protected when you invest them through the diocese. Plus, you can be assured of a good rate of return.

I'd be remiss if I didn't also mention the importance of communications with the diocese. If there's anything big going in your parish—anything you think is kind of extraordinary or perhaps tragic—tell someone in the diocese. Keep the lines of communication open. Don't let the archbishop or the bishop read about it first in the newspaper. They're not likely to be too pleased.

The Parish Council

I'd like to switch gears slightly and offer some observations on parish resources, such as the parish council. This body should serve as your planning council. You should, of course, have a long-range plan, and who's better equipped to help you develop this blueprint than the parish council? Its members were either elected or cajoled by you into serving. Either way, they know the parish. Having served as a pastor and chancery officer, my strong advice to you is to make sure the chairs of both your parish council and finance council think like you do and that they have your vision for the parish. If they don't, they can cause you problems. If it does get to that point, you need to have a conversation with the chair to try to bring him or her around. We tend to use our hearts and not our heads in dealing with people. But the reality is, you have a job to do.

You've got a parish that you want to be a great Christian community, and if people are preventing you from accomplishing that goal, then you have to take a firm stand and have the courage of your conviction.

Who you have on your councils will indeed be critical to their success. Certainly have accountants on your finance council, but be aware they are often narrow in their scope and won't allow you a lot of flexibility on issues.

Identifying Potential Leaders

It's undoubtedly clear today that personnel matters are among the toughest challenges you'll face as pastors. They're a sensitive area you must deal with constantly, and they touch on not just paid staff but volunteers as well. Volunteers present their own set of challenges, since it's twice as hard sometimes to fire volunteers or move them out. Personnel decisions get to the much broader issue of leadership and how you mitigate problems with people who are nonproductive or standing in the way of progress. Good leaders know how to identify other potential leaders. And the larger your organization, the more potential leaders you have. So, focus on singling out talented and promising individuals who can be moved into leadership roles to replace those in your organization who aren't producing. And then bring these promising individuals along. If they do a good job on a project, give them another with more responsibility. You'll be pleasantly surprised to find how well these emerging leaders take the ball and run with it.

The Necessity of Raising Money

There are limits, of course, to what any one pastor can do, and so you'll have to bring in consultants once in awhile. A case in point is raising money—which nobody likes to do. Some advice I can give you here is, don't get up in the pulpit and say to the congregation, "You know what, I hate to ask you for money. I didn't get ordained for that." Guess what? You did. So don't apologize. I ask people for money constantly—every day of the week, at breakfast, lunch, and dinner. Do I like it? No. Do I do it? Absolutely. That persistence enabled us at St. Thomas University to just finish a fifty-million-dollar capital campaign.

As you'll quickly learn, it's your fiduciary responsibility as pastor to keep your parish resourced.

The SWOT Analysis

Having a plan for your parish is extremely important. It is your road map to a successful future. In doing your planning, the first thing you should undertake is a SWOT Analysis. That is an analysis of your strengths, your weaknesses, your opportunities, and your threats. For example, the strength of your parish may be in its financial position, or it may be in the involvement of the people in the parish, or it may be the history of the parish and esprit de corps of those who once belonged to the parish. A weakness might be changing leadership. Perhaps the pastor has changed three times in the last three years, and you're now down to one parochial vicar from two. An opportunity—which is a problem not easy but still possible to overcome—might be the fact you have no Sunday evening Mass. A threat could be a change in demographics or the declining population of your school.

As pastor, you're the one with a vision for the parish and who will go in with some thoughts about what you would like the parish to do. For example, you might want it to be more involved with community outreach, or helping underserved populations, or deepening the spiritual life of families. If what you want the parish to become is your vision, then what your parish does at the present time is its mission. The mission is what you would put on your website to attract people. For example, you might describe yourselves as "an active parish with many ministries, a children's Mass, and vibrant liturgies." Your vision builds on the current mission.

In the course of your planning, determine three to five things you would like to accomplish in the next five years. These are your goals. Break your goals into manageable objectives. Create benchmarks for where you are now and where you want to be next year. Put a schedule together and a budget. Assess your plans. And each year evaluate your successes. Did you meet the objectives you set forth? If not, find out why. Perhaps the objectives weren't attainable. You might also have to reshape your goals.

Planning should always be done by a group. As I mentioned above, your parish council is an ideal planning group. I suggest that you have a yearly meeting, a kind of retreat, focused on your plan, and if the planning committee is the parish council, a retreat is also a good time to get the council members' thoughts on how you're doing with the parish in general. Your goals should be *smart*: they should be specific, measurable, achievable, realistic, and time-bound. As far as specificity is concerned, make sure your objectives are concrete, detailed, focused, action-oriented, and simple, and identify who should be doing things. Make sure you are realistic about your possible achievements and set deadlines.

Wear a Happy Face

My final piece of advice has nothing to do with the Pastoral Center. Just be a happy pastor and stay positive. When I was a pastor and vicar general at the same time, a somewhat stressful situation as you might imagine, I found great support in meeting monthly with a group of priests, most of whom were pastors or, like me, heavily engaged in diocesan activities. We used the opportunity to discuss ways in which we could improve our parishes, and usually we did it based on readings we had recommended to one another. Our conversations were constructive, positive, and energizing.

Being a pastor ought to be an enjoyable experience. It does have its headaches, but it also has tremendous rewards. Your people will love you, and they'll provide you with enormous satisfactions by bringing you into their homes and their families, and they'll respect you because you are a competent leader of their Christian community. Happy pastors usually get the respect of other priests and bishops, as well, to say nothing of what the Lord has in store for those of us who pastor his people well.

Endnotes

1. Second Vatican Council, *Christus Dominus* (Decree concerning the Pastoral Office of Bishops in the Church), 1965.

15

In Pursuit of Priestly Well-Being

Paul S. Manning

Like many of you, I've had to negotiate priesthood from a variety of jobs and ministries. I've served as a parochial vicar in a suburban parish; as a chaplain, teacher, and president in one of our diocesan high schools; as diocesan vocation director; and, most recently, as vicar for education and pastor. After twenty-five years, I'm still feeling pretty well (and hopefully presenting the same way) which is why, I hope, I was asked to address the subject of priestly well-being.

Generally speaking, I've learned two important things from my experience with the priesthood and formation. The first is that all of us are neurotic in some way, striving for integration, for holiness. We all have quirks we need to work on. Being "well" doesn't exempt us from being imperfect, from being "in process," from still being inescapably "human."

The second thing I've learned is, there are many priests and pastors who do priesthood well, and that is certainly a possibility for all of us. In fact, God's plan for us is that we *do* priesthood well. I'd refer you to Jeremiah 29:11: "For I know well the plans I have in mind for you . . . plans for your welfare and not for woe" (NABRE). So, God's deep desire for us—his active work on our behalf—is for our welfare.

I don't present myself as an expert on wellness, however, but as a brother priest and pastor convinced of God's desire for our well-being. Some valuable resources on priestly life and priestly well-being—some older, some newer—are worth referencing. First is *Quickening the Fire in Our Midst*, by George Aschenbrenner, a Jesuit priest who has engaged in spiritual direction with diocesan priests for many years and who writes of his experiences. The result is a very good book on priestly spirituality.[1]

Another great resource is a book written a number of years ago by Fr. Donald Cozzens, *The Spirituality of the Diocesan Priest.*[2] A more recent and very practical book is *The Joy of Priesthood,* by Fr. Stephen Rosetti, who's affiliated with St. Luke's Institute and its work with priests and their wellness.[3] A book not as well-known but equally as insightful is a little handbook on psychological and spiritual integration titled *How to Be an Adult* by David Richo.[4] I love to pick this book up every now and then and use its checklists to ask myself if I'm getting out of sync or losing balance, especially in my relationships with people.

And finally, I want to mention two excellent books that somebody put in my hands when I was in the seminary: *Being Sexual and Celibate* and *An Experience of Celibacy.*[5] Both were written in the 1980s by a Capuchin Franciscan named Keith Clark and are still helpful today in trying to understand what celibacy is and how to live it in a healthy way.

Jesus' Concern for Our Well-Being

It is useful to start with a working definition of "well-being." The Oxford Online Dictionary defines well-being as the state of being comfortable, healthy, or happy. On the basis of that definition, I would pose the question: "Is Jesus concerned about our well-being as priests?"

On the one hand, our answer might be "no." Our position would be that Jesus' focus on self-denial and the abandonment of material comforts and concerns means that well-being is not an important subject for him. He encourages dying to self. On the other hand, our answer might be "yes." Here our position would be that after Jesus sent his disciples out two-by-two, he called them back and told them they needed a period of rest and refreshment in their lives. So other evidence suggests that Jesus *was* concerned about the well-being of his disciples.

Which again invites the question: is Jesus concerned about our well-being as priests? My response is that Jesus' concern for healing, for health, for the wholeness of his people demonstrated so regularly in his healing ministry, suggests that he *is* concerned about our well-being. I think about his statement, "You shall love the Lord, your God, with all your mind, with all your heart, with all your soul, with all your strength," that is, with your whole self. I think we can reasonably say that if Jesus desires health and wholeness for his people, then by extension that would apply to his priests, as well.

It's helpful to consider another definition of well-being, like the one found on the U.S. Army website, of all places. Well-being is defined there as "the personal, physical, material, mental and spiritual state of soldiers, civilians and their families that contributes to their preparedness to perform the Army's mission."

So, for the U.S. Army, the well-being of its soldiers is tightly linked to its mission. Which makes me wonder, should this definition be applied to the priesthood as well? In light of this definition, if the question is posed, "Should we be concerned as priests about our well-being as a primary goal, or as our sole agenda," then the answer is no. But if the question becomes, "Should we be concerned about the well-being, wholeness, and holiness of God's *people* as a primary goal," then the answer is yes. Are we part of these people? Again, the answer is yes, which makes it fair to conclude that Jesus is concerned about our well-being as disciples and as priests; he's concerned about our well-being insofar as it serves the mission of the kingdom, which is wholeness for his people.

What I'm suggesting is that we want to look at and expend some energy reflecting on and pursuing our well-being, but since it's a relative good for us as priests, it shouldn't be our primary goal.

Years ago, when I was conducting Pre-Cana sessions with couples in our parish as a young priest, I remember asking my mom and dad how long they thought couples should wait before having children. And my parents, who had ten children, said they wouldn't wait too long to bring another person into the world for one very good reason: a child takes the focus off yourself and whether or not your needs and expectations are being met by the other person in the relationship, and puts the focus on the needs of the newborn. I think there's wisdom here for the priesthood as well. The truth is, we can become overly concerned about our well-being. How often do we ask the question, "Am I happy where I am and with what I'm doing?" I'd suggest that this is not the primary question or concern we ought to have. At the very least, Jesus wants health, wholeness, and holiness for his people, his disciples, and he wants priests who will foster that. To that end, Jesus is concerned about our well-being, especially our emotional and spiritual well-being. In other words, Jesus is concerned about our well-being to the extent that it serves the well-being of his people. We should be as concerned as Jesus is about our own well-being—no more, no less—not as an end in itself, but as a means to serving the well-being of his people.

Reflecting on the Rite of Ordination

Knowing, then, that priestly well-being is a valid (though relative) concern, where do we look to reflect on priestly life and well-being? I'd like to suggest three places for theological reflection on the shape and structure of the priestly life. The first is the Scriptures. The second is the sacraments and liturgy, the *lex orandi* of the church. And the third is the magisterial teachings on priesthood.

The Scriptures are obviously worth studying when trying to determine the outline of a priestly life well-lived. Especially fruitful is a reflection on Luke's accounts of the call and commissioning of apostles and the seventy-two disciples, especially his instruction to take neither walking stick, nor sandals, nor traveling bag (Luke 9:3). What a meaningful place to reflect on what these things mean in terms of a priestly life. What exactly *are* the walking stick, sandals, and traveling bags in our lives that Jesus prohibits?

There is also a trove of worthwhile and provocative material in the church's magisterial teachings. Two of our most recent popes, John Paul II and Benedict, have reflected deeply and written extensively on the priesthood.

But the place I'd really like to focus on—an unlikely place, perhaps, when it comes to reflecting on the priestly life over the long-term—is the Rite of Ordination.

We've all experienced this rite. It's meant to constitute us in the priestly life and to establish our priestly identity. The defining moments in that rite are instructive, formational, memorable, and, of course, sacramental. Their impact stays with us forever. In my own ordination, two specific moments stand out in my mind: one is sitting among the people and listening to my brother (in this case, my actual twin brother Peter) proclaim the First Reading. And the other moment, which caught me off-guard and caused me to take a deep breath, occurred at the end of the Mass when the bishop asked for my first blessing as a priest. After I blessed him, he took my hands and kissed my palms, and I remember being startled by that moment and realizing that something big and important had just happened to me.

These are the two physical moments etched in my memory. On Good Friday, when I lie prostrate before the altar, I always think of my ordination, of when the bishop kissed the palms of my hands. One might say that I have a "muscle memory" of that experience. What do I mean by "muscle memory"? Golfers typically talk about muscle memory; if you practice your swing enough, there comes a point at which your muscles remember the movement and you don't have to think about your swing anymore.

I would like to suggest that we should have a muscle memory of the Rite of Ordination so that it can help us live our priestly lives. Indeed, I think it was designed to accomplish just that.

Are the actions of the Rite of Ordination really a legitimate way to instruct us in the outlines of a priestly life? Two passages in the *Catechism of the Catholic Church* respond affirmatively to that question. The first reads:

> The Holy Spirit gives a spiritual understanding of the Word of God to those who read or hear it, according to the dispositions of their hearts. By means of the words, actions, and symbols that form the structure of a celebration, the Spirit puts both the faithful and the ministers into a living relationship with Christ, the Word and Image of the Father, so that they can live out the meaning of what they hear, contemplate, and do in the celebration. (§ 1101)

Note what it says here: the actions of a sacramental celebration can help us live out the meaning of what we do in the celebration.

The second passage is:

> A sacramental celebration is a meeting of God's children with their Father, in Christ and the Holy Spirit; this meeting takes the form of a dialogue, through actions and words. Admittedly, the symbolic actions are already a language, but the Word of God and the response of faith have to accompany and give life to them, so that the seed of the Kingdom can bear its fruit in good soil. The liturgical actions signify what the Word of God expresses: both his free initiative and his people's response of faith. (§ 1153)

So a sacramental celebration is a meeting of God's people with him, and the meeting takes the form of a "*dialogue*, through *actions* and words" (emphasis added).

These two passages express a conviction that the sacraments form us and that their words, symbols, and actions can be lived, that is, give us "a way of life." They express a conviction that the *physical* dimension of the sacraments, the actions (even before the words are spoken) have deep meaning, that they "speak."

With that in mind, I'd like to explore with you the stances we took as candidates at our ordinations and what they say about the long-term "postures" we ought to be taking in our priestly lives. We will focus on the ongoing priestly characteristics that are called for and their potentially harmful opposites. And we will suggest concrete practices to engender those characteristics in our own lives.

Familiarity as a Long-Term Goal

The first posture in the Rite of Ordination is *seated in view of the faithful*. For those of us ordained before 2002, the instructions were clear: all candidates should be seated among the people of God. The faithful are a primary focus of this celebration, and those to be ordained enjoy membership in the family of the baptized within the church. What, then, is the priestly characteristic that flows from this, which needs to be lived out over the long-term? That characteristic is the capacity for relationships: sociability and familiarity. The priest needs familiarity with trusted laypeople. By way of comparison, the antitheses of these qualities would be isolation or exclusivity.

A cautionary note about familiarity is in order here. Our intimacy with others needs to be with those who will help us honor our commitment to the priesthood. In his books *Being Sexual and Celibate* and *An Experience of Celibacy*, Keith Clark talks about how commitments evolve. When we make ourselves transparent to another, he writes, that person begins to invest in us. And when we share deeply with another and that person becomes transparent in return, a commitment starts to evolve. It's in the evolution of commitments that we need to be really careful, according to Clark. When we begin to share our feelings about the other person and start to elicit from that person his or her feelings about us, the agenda becomes the relationship, and a commitment begins to evolve. And before we realize what's happening, we may be into a commitment that starts to pull us away from our priestly mission.

The point is this: we need to be careful about transparency, and if we're going to share our feelings for others, we need to do that with a trusted ally who's going to help us honor our commitment to the priesthood. I believe a key question to ask ourselves is this: are we beginning to see our future in terms of this other person? If the answer is yes, then we have begun to step over the line to where our future, our well-being, is predicated on this relationship with the other person.

The Importance of Accountability

Another posture we took as candidates at our ordination was to *stand before the bishop*, who questioned us. We did that, though, in the presence of the people, signifying that I'm elected from among others, that I'm chosen, summoned, or called from this crowd. As for the significance of that to our long-term priestly lives and to our well-being, it suggests that we ought to, as a result, possess a healthy self-confidence and self-awareness in ministry. Its opposite would be neediness.

Another meaning that is suggested by standing before the bishop and being questioned by him is that we as priests ought to be—and, in fact, are—subject to scrutiny. And what priestly quality should we embrace in our lives to respond to the act of being scrutinized? One answer is accountability. Fr. Stephen Rosetti advises applying the "grandmother rule," which states, "Never do anything that your grandmother would be embarrassed by."

Scrutiny also implies the need for feedback from others. Just as we stood before the bishop during the Rite of Ordination, we stand before our congregation and the public in our pastoral roles and need to be made fully aware of anything we do that's untoward or inappropriate. That is where the *fraternal imperative* of the priestly life, which was given to us by Jesus, can be quite beneficial.

What is the fraternal imperative? Consider the fact that Jesus on at least two occasions called a set of brothers to discipleship and apostleship, revealing and illuminating a deeper spiritual necessity among those who served him in the circle of the Twelve. And that necessity is that they ought to be brothers. He calls them as such, and they see one another as such, as evidenced in the Acts of the Apostles and in their letters. Among those who share Jesus' ministry as apostles and coworkers, there is a fraternal imperative.

My experience has been that healthy priests have one or two close friends in the priesthood with whom they are brothers, or kindred spirits, and with whom they can share things they wouldn't share with others. To be sure, there is an association, a camaraderie, with the wider community of priests, but there are probably only a couple within that fraternity whom you can truly call brothers. They constitute a vital and necessary set of relationships (hence the term "fraternal imperative") in every priest's life.

Never Stop Teaching

The third posture we took during ordination was to *sit before the bishop*, who addressed us on the duties of priesthood. We, as candidates, are being taught by the bishop and, by extension, the church. And the enduring priestly skill we should take away from this posture is to be students and teachers ourselves throughout our ministries.

When I was a young priest, I got invited to do talks all the time. I found that once I had been around for awhile and had ridden the circuit, once I had become an administrator and a pastor and my hair had turned gray, I didn't get quite the same number of invitations. But I firmly believe we still have to keep ourselves in a teaching mode. So, I continue to make presentations for Pre-Cana and the RCIA and try to visit our local elementary school. I continue to work with our young people in confirmation, despite my having passed the age of relevance to them.

The reason I maintain an active teaching profile is that it forces me to learn; it compels me to be a good listener. Some priests, as they move into other ministries and the later stages of their lives, get tired of doing talks and the research that's required to do them well. But a healthy priestly life doesn't allow that. Effective priests continue to be active teachers as well as eager learners and listeners. And they look for opportunities to engage in these pursuits throughout their careers, recognizing that their well-being in no small way depends on it.

Obedience to the Church

The fourth posture in the ordination experience is the act of *kneeling before the bishop*. It happens a number of times, the first being when the newly ordained kneels and places his joined hands between the bishop's hands. The significance of this, obviously, is obedience. Its opposite would be independence, but not in a healthy sense.

Obedience is particularly important for the priest to embrace and emulate because to do otherwise models a lack of regard for legitimate authority—of state, parents, teachers, and the church. If a priest starts to undermine by his demeanor and his actions the respect and authority that are due the bishop and his office, then he detracts—without perhaps realizing it—from the obedience owed to every role of authority within the church. It makes little sense to be negative about the bishop and refuse to follow his lead, and then expect our staff and people in the parish to give us *their* respect and obedience.

Other times that the priest kneels before the bishop are when the bishop anoints his hands with chrism, and again when the bishop hands him the paten and chalice. Here, the actions of the rite speak of the priest's identity with Christ, the Anointed One, who is also the one who breaks himself and pours himself out, the one who entrusts himself into our hands. These actions require a priestly life that identifies with Christ and intimately experiences him, especially in terms of leadership in and at the Eucharist. Some seemingly opposite characteristics are required here—for example, an acceptance of and comfort with responsibility and "power," versus a subordination to Christ and the humility and vulnerability that come with entrusting oneself to others. In most cases, it was this deep and real experience of the powerful Christ and the humble Christ that drew us to our vocation.

While our discussion has touched on some of the most poignant stances and postures of the Rite of Ordination, there are certainly others worthy of reflection. As my final thought, I encourage you to seek them out, for it is by probing the meaning, characteristics, and practices inherent in each of these actions that we can continue to gain valuable insights into, and hopefully embrace, those qualities that are vital to a priestly life well-lived.

Endnotes

1. George A. Aschenbrenner, *Quickening the Fire in Our Midst* (Chicago: Loyola Press, 2002).

2. Donald B. Cozzens, *The Spirituality of the Diocesan Priest* (Collegeville, MN: Liturgical Press, 1997).

3. Stephen J. Rosetti, *The Joy of Priesthood* (Notre Dame, IN: Ave Maria Press, 2005).

4. David Richo, *How to Be an Adult* (Mahwah, NJ: Paulist Press, 2002).

5. Keith Clark, *Being Sexual and Celibate* (Notre Dame, IN: Ave Maria Press, 1986); *An Experience of Celibacy: A Creative Reflection on Intimacy, Loneliness, Sexuality and Commitment* (Notre Dame, IN: Ave Maria Press, 1982).

Performance Improvement Memo

Subject:
From:
Date:

On the above date, I spoke with the above employee in the presence of and (if applicable) regarding:

The issue:

I have asked the employee to:

Date by which corrective action should be accomplished:

The following action will be taken if improvement in this area does not occur within the prescribed time frame:

Employee comments (optional):

_____   _____
Supervisor/Manager   Date

_____   _____
Employee   Date

The employee's signature serves only to acknowledge that this matter has been discussed with him/her. It does not necessarily indicate agreement with this action.

Appendix B

Total Compensation

Introduction

A paycheck is the most visible piece of an employee's compensation. S/he receives it every other week or perhaps bimonthly. However, it is very easy for an employee to overlook the other costs associated with his or her employment, some of which provide nontaxable benefits, that the employer pays. And why not? These are numbers they usually don't see. But they represent a significant cost to your school and/or parish.

So, as part of your recruiting (and ongoing employee communication) efforts, you should make employees aware of their <u>total compensation</u>.

In the box below is a sample of part of an offer letter that does just this. Assumptions:
- Annual salary was $38,000.
- Individual was expected to choose individual health coverage.

Benefits added <u>an additional</u> 35% to the employee's compensation, raising it to almost $51,500. (If your school or parish pays 100% of the health insurance premium, as some do, the number is even higher).

From the offer letter or letter of appointment:
However, compensation is more than just salary. As a school that is part of the Diocese of Knoxville, we offer generous benefits. Following is more detail on those benefits.

Benefits	School's cost (annual $)	Your cost (annual $)
Medical, dental, and vision insurance	$7,785	$410
Life, long-term disability, and accidental death and dismemberment insurance	117	0
Two retirement plans		
• *Defined benefit plan.* Four percent of your annual salary	1,520	0
• *Defined contribution plan* should you choose to participate: 100% match up to 3% of your salary	1,140	1,140
Social Security	2,907	2,907
Total	$13,469	

These mostly nontaxable benefits add an additional 35% to your base salary, for a total compensation of $51,469 (not counting vacation and workers' compensation premium).

Appendix C

Procedures of the Office of Conciliation
Archdiocese of Saint Paul and Minneapolis

Introduction

This is my Commandment: Love one another as I have loved you.

John 15:13

God's presence is found and reflected in our love of God and one another. It is through love and faith that the mission of our Church—to accept the Reign of God in our lives—is accomplished. When we are in conflict with each other, and with those organizations that seek to serve the common good, there is a fundamental spiritual and social need to resolve such conflict.

The Office of Conciliation serves those individuals and organizations in conflict who seek reconciliation in a manner that embraces Christ's presence, the rich legacy of the Scriptures, and the principles of Catholic social teaching.

In fulfilling its mission, the Office of Conciliation recognizes four key principles of Catholic social teaching: the value and dignity of the human person, the common good, participation and justice. By applying these principles, we seek a unified relationship among individuals and organizations.

> • **The value and dignity of the human person.** The most important aspect of human activity lies beyond what is produced or achieved. It is the extent to which that activity reflects and promotes human dignity. Individuals need to evaluate how well their activities serve their life and God. Organizations must evaluate their environment and expectations in light of an individual's reasonable aspirations and needs.

• **Common Good.** While standing for and supporting the value of the individual, individuals and organizations also focus on the larger society to promote the common good as well. The notion of the common good is complex and multi-faceted. It "embraces the sum more readily to achieve their own fulfillment." (John XXIII, Mater et Magistra ["Mother and Teacher"], 1961) It encompasses more than material wellbeing. The Church adds an important spiritual dimension in its contribution to the common good.

• **Participation.** Participation brings together the interests of the individual and the common good. The individual is respected as a person. The input of many individuals helps the organization move in appropriate directions in pursuit of the common good. Participation is a tapestry of collegiality, collaboration, and consultation.

• **Justice.** The word "justice" derives from the concept of "right relationships." Justice occurs when individuals contribute conscientiously to human and organizational relationships, and when organizations establish policies and systems that elevate human dignity. Justice recognizes the existence of certain fundamental rights and freedoms which we share equally, including (1) respect for one's person, and the right to protect one's person and privacy, (2) the right to be informed of proposed actions which affect one's rights, (3) the right to be heard in defense of one's rights, and to address one's accusers, and (4) the right to be judged fairly and impartially.[1]

In seeking to resolve conflicts that interfere with our relationship with God and with each other, the Office of Conciliation acknowledges God's presence throughout the processes of conciliation and arbitration. The Office encourages all participants in these processes to embrace the following principles:

- that we acknowledge Christ's presence in this process, in discourse and in prayer;
- that we be respectful in speech and manner;
- that we strive to open our hearts to the needs and voices of others, in the spirit of good will and justice;
- that we recognize that no law can be as compelling as Christ's commandment to love one another; and
- that we recognize that the ultimate goal is to find Christ and His love for us through reconciliation with Him and each other.

The Office of Conciliation offers its services as a simple and readily accessible response to human conflicts, with the hope that it will help the people of this Archdiocese to abide by Christ's commandment and to accept and establish the Reign of God.

The Office of Conciliation offers two methods to resolve conflicts:

1) Conciliation

In conciliation, the parties are the agents of reaching a just resolution of the conflict, with the assistance of an experienced, impartial conciliator approved by the parties. The object of conciliation is for the parties to work together to develop a just resolution. The proposed resolution must be accepted by both of the parties in order to be a binding agreement. In this process the conciliator assists the parties in developing proposals for resolution, but does not have the authority to impose a solution without the agreement of the parties.

The Office of Conciliation encourages parties to seek resolution through this process, because persons of good will, committed to the Gospel spirit of love and reconciliation, can often find resolution with the assistance of another committed to that same spirit.

2) Arbitration

Because not all conflicts can be resolved through conciliation, arbitration is also offered. In arbitration, those in conflict agree to allow an experienced, impartial arbitrator approved by the parties to resolve the conflict. Arbitration adds the important element of the readiness of the parties to accept the decision of the arbitrator as final and binding.[2]

Endnotes

1. Statement of Purpose of the Office of Conciliation, Archdiocese of Saint Paul and Minneapolis, http://www.archspm.org/departments/conciliation/purpose.php.

2. Procedures of the Office of Conciliation, Archdiocese of Saint Paul and Minneapolis, revised April 23, 2013, http://www.archspm.org/_uls/resources/Manual-of-Procedures-2013-04-23.pdf

Contributors

David Boettner was ordained a priest for the Diocese of Knoxville in 1994 and currently serves as its moderator of the curia and vicar general, as well as pastor of Sacred Heart Cathedral which has seventeen hundred families and a school pre-K to 8th grade with over six hundred students. In his roles with the diocesan offices and the cathedral parish, Fr. Boettner oversees more than one hundred full-time employees as well as many volunteers.

Michael Brough is director of strategic engagement for the National Leadership Roundtable on Church Management. An experienced presenter and teacher, he was a member of the RENEW International Service Team, serving as its director from 2001-06. With master's degrees in anthropology and pastoral studies, he has worked with and trained lay ecclesial ministers in dioceses and parishes across the United States and in twelve countries.

Franklyn Casale, president of St. Thomas University in Florida since 1994, writes about the pastor and his relationship to the diocese. Prior to his university presidency, Msgr. Casale served as the vicar general, chancellor, and moderator of the curia of the Newark archdiocese.

Arturo Chávez is president of the Mexican American Catholic College in San Antonio. He has worked for over three decades as a teacher, youth minister, chaplain to the incarcerated, and community organizer. Nationally recognized for his efforts to combat racism and poverty, he was appointed by President Barack Obama to serve as an advisor on the White House Council for Faith Based and Community Partnerships. Catholic Charities USA recognized him as a "national champion of the poor" with the "Keep the Dream Alive Award" in honor of the Rev. Dr. Martin Luther King, Jr.

Dennis Corcoran is pastoral associate for Church of Christ the King in New Vernon, NJ. For many years, he was a pastoral associate and director of operations at Church of the Presentation in Saddle River, NJ. He has spoken across the country on many topics, including liturgy, stewardship, and church management.

Thomas J. Healey is Treasurer of the National Leadership Roundtable on Church Management and a Senior Fellow at Harvard University's John F. Kennedy School of Government. He joined Goldman, Sachs & Co. in 1985 and became a partner in 1988. He also served as Assistant Secretary of the U.S. Treasury for Domestic Finance under Ronald Reagan. On the board of Foundations and Donors Interested in Catholic Activities (FADICA), he is a Chartered Financial Analyst and a Counselor of Real Estate and, with Roger Porter and Robert Glauber, he co-edited *New Directions in Financial Regulation*, a book that discusses the 2008 financial crisis.

Paul A. Holmes is Distinguished University Professor of Servant Leadership, teaching moral and sacramental theology at Seton Hall University. He had been a member of the President's executive cabinet for ten years holding the titles of vice president for mission and ministry, vice president and interim dean of Seton Hall's School of Diplomacy and International Relations, and executive vice president. Ordained for the Archdiocese of Newark, he has been at Seton Hall since 1988.

Jim Lundholm-Eades is director of services and planning at the National Leadership Roundtable for Church Management, having worked in multiple fields for over thirty-six years, both in his native Australia and in the United States. With degrees in counseling, pastoral counseling, educational administration, and business administration, he has published work (and videos) on church management, strategic planning, and effective presbyteral councils. He has also taught graduate-level courses in strategic planning, administration, and stewardship, and Catholic school finance at the Murray Institute of the University of St. Thomas in Minneapolis.

John McGovern is a licensed CPA, holds the designation of Personal Financial Specialist and is also a Certified Financial Planner and a Registered Investment Advisor with the Securities and Exchange Commission. He began his career with Deloitte and Touche, and in 1986 opened his accounting practice specializing in the areas of tax, investment management, and church accounting. Currently, John provides accounting services to thirty parishes, cemeteries, and parish schools.

Paul S. Manning was ordained in 1985 for the Diocese of Paterson and is currently the Vicar for Evangelization at St. Paul Inside the Walls, the Paterson Diocesan Center for Evangelization. Before his appointment as pastor and vicar for education, Fr. Manning served many years as a parish priest, the diocesan vocation director, and the chaplain and president of Morris Catholic High School.

Maria Mendoza was the business manager at St. Rose of Lima parish in East Hanover, NJ. With an MBA from Babson College, she worked at Ernst & Young and Drexel Burnham & Lambert investment firms.

Kerry A. Robinson is executive director of the National Leadership Roundtable on Church Management and also serves on the Board of Directors of FADICA (Foundations and Donors Interested in Catholic Activities). She is also on the advisory boards of the Center of Church Management at Villanova University and the Institute for Religious Education and Pastoral Ministry at Boston College. She wrote *Imagining Abundance: Fundraising, Philanthropy, and a Spiritual Call to Service* (Liturgical Press, 2014).

Robert Stagg has been a priest of the Archdiocese of Newark since 1975. He has been a pastor of two vibrant parishes over the last fifteen years and is presently shepherding Our Lady of Presentation Parish in Upper Saddle River, NJ. He was an adjunct instructor of homiletics for ten years at Newark's Immaculate Conception Seminary and was director of Campus Ministry, 1981–1994, at Caldwell College. Fr. Stagg is an engaging speaker with insights based on a wealth of experience.

Jack Wall was an innovative and well-respected pastor of Chicago's historic Old St. Patrick's Church in Chicago's West Loop for two and a half decades. In 2007 the Holy See appointed him president of the Catholic Church Extension Society, a national organization that strengthens the Church's presence and mission in under-resourced and isolated communities across the United States.

Charles E. Zech is a professor of economics at Villanova University and is the director of the Center for the Study of Church Management there. With a PHD from Notre Dame University, he is the author or co-author of over seventy-five books and articles, including *Money Matters: Personal Giving in American Churches; The Parish Management Handbook; Lay Ministers and Their Spiritual Practices; Listening to the People of God: Closing, Rebuilding, and Revitalizing Parishes;* and *Best Practices in Parish Stewardship.*